From Emptiness to Empowerment

Changing Physical and Other Losses into Strengths

by

Brian J. Hubbard, LICSW

DORRANCE PUBLISHING CO., INC.
PITTSBURGH, PENNSYLVANIA 15222

"In *From Emptiness to Empowerment,* Brian Hubbard draws on his numerous contacts, own experience, and extensive training to write a book that will help numerous people, whether or not they consider themselves as having a disability. It clearly delineates the steps people can take to take charge of their life, pull themselves up by their bootstraps, and become 'king of their own mountain.' I recommend it heartily, particularly for people with disabilities who are feeling overwhelmed by their situation. Pour yourself a cup of coffee, sit down in your favorite chair, and enjoy."

Phillip Zazove, M.D., of the University of Michigan
Author of *When the Phone Rings, My Bed Shakes*

"I certainly admire what you're [Brian Hubbard] accomplishing and wish you the best of luck in your work and coming publications."

Leon Uris
Author of *Trinity*

ISBN #0-8059-4010-3
Printed in the United States of America

First Printing

For information or to order additional books, please write:
Dorrance Publishing Co., Inc.
643 Smithfield Street
Pittsburgh, Pennsylvania 15222
U.S.A.

Dedication

I would like to dedicate this book to all friends and supporters that made Counseling for Independent Living, my personal and professional dream, become a reality, specifically board members Bob O'Neill, Chris Kinder, Lee Hussey, Frank Zweir, and Dan Noyes. A special thanks goes to U.S. Senators Claiborne Pell and John Chafee as well as their staff for their major contributions and support. Congressman Patrick Kennedy, a friend as well as a supporter, has contributed countless hours in helping out CIL, as well as Salty Brine, one of Rhode Island's most renowned figures. They must be included in this dedication.

CIL most likely would not have become a reality without the visibility I acquired as a former member of the U.S. Disabled Ski Team, and thus supporters of that effort are part of this dedication as well. This includes my loyal friends from my hometown of Lynn, Massachusetts: Ray and Nackie Bastarache, Gary Bogart, Frank and Judy Cause, Harold and Karen McGaughey, and Larry and Wendy Pleau. Jess Kane, D.M.D., an old college buddy, played a major role in this as well.

Acknowledgments

Writing a book without sight is a big enough challenge to begin with—one needs to rely on hearing to listen to recorded transcriptions, and when this hearing is severely impaired, the challenge even becomes greater. Thus the reliance on the support of friends and professional staff alike becomes a primary requirement. This happens to be the case for me in the "writing" of this book. The book never would have been possible without the support and help of friends and staff alike. The help provided by these people is a clear example of the constructive use of support systems discussed in later sections of this book, and it would be a grave injustice for them not to be recognized for their invaluable contributions. I would like to thank Jim and Cindy Killavey (Jimcin Recordings, Portsmouth RI), as well as Ethel Chafton for their countless hours of reading printed text into audio recordings. My good friend, Frank Zweir, literally spent days with me in doing the same with his unselfish dedication. Kate Imbrie, widowed wife of one of my closest friends (who passed away around the time of this book's publication) was also invaluable with her review and support. I would like to thank the people with me at Counseling for Independent Living, particularly Beth Guerra and Julie Miller for their encouragement and invaluable help with reading, transcribing, word-processing, typing, and editing. I would also like to thank the staff at Dorrance Publishing Co., Inc. for their technical editing and guidance, as well as thanks to my literary agents, Tony Seidl and John Holmes, for their guidance. I would like to express my most grateful appreciation, however, to Evelyn Morrison and Linda Bernard for their sacrifice of many hours in the editing and transcribing of the original manuscript. They asked for nothing in return and their unselfish generosity is an example of healthy support systems on the authentic, spiritual level. I also wish to thank Karen Escalera for her extensive help as well. A special thanks to my wife, Judy. Although we sadly had to go in different directions, her strong encouragement was invaluable.

My deepest appreciation, however, goes to the hundreds of clients I have served in the past twenty years, especially those disabled individuals that I served at Counseling for Independent Living in the last seven years, for their hard work, courage, and dedication to change through the use of psychotherapy has given me the major inspiration to write this book.

On Joy and Sorrow:

"...Your joy is your sorrow unmasked. And the self same well from which your laughter rises was oftentimes filled with your tears. And how else can it be? The deeper that sorrow carves into your being, the more joy you can contain. Is not the cup that holds your wine the very cup that was burned in the potter's oven? And is not the lute that soothes your spirit, the very wood that was hollowed with knives? When you are joyous, look deep into your heart and you shall find it is only that which has given you sorrow that is giving you joy. When you are sorrowful look again in your heart, and you shall see that in truth you are weeping for that which has been your delight."

The Prophet by Kahlil Gibran

"What is real?" asked the Rabbit one day. "Does it mean you have things stuffed inside you, or a stick or a handle?"

"Real isn't how you are made," said the Skin Horse. "It's a thing that happens to you. When a child loves you for a long, long time, not just to play with, but really loves you, then you become real."

"Does it hurt?" asked the Rabbit.

"Sometimes," said the Skin Horse. "When you are real, you don't mind being hurt."

"Does it happen all at once, or is it like being wound up bit by bit?" (Rabbit)

"It doesn't happen all at once, you become. It takes a long time. That's why it doesn't happen often to people who break easily or have sharp edges, or who you have to be careful of when you touch." "Generally by the time you are real, most of your hair has been loved off, and your eyes drop out." "You get loose at the joints and very shabby." "But these things don't matter at all, because once you are real you can't be ugly, except to people who don't matter." (Skin Horse)

The Velveteen Rabbit by Margery Williams

"Nothing then is unchangeable but the inherent and inalienable rights of man."

Thomas Jefferson

"The word power has a two-fold meaning. One is the possession of power over somebody, the ability to dominate him. The other meaning is to do something, to be able to be potent...We do not think of a person who is not able to dominate others but of a person who is not able to do what he wants (powerlessness)."

Escape From Freedom by Erich Fromm

Introduction

While it may appear that the major theme in this book is that of disability issues, the real theme is a central issue in anyone's life—dealing with losses. Because living for anyone is always a challenging process, a major component of successful living simply is the ability to confront change and, thus, losses by letting go or giving up old ideas and behaviors in the pursuit of growth. This book essentially has relevance for anyone who is a member of the human race. While it appears that the primary focus group in this book is disabled individuals, this focus group is only a representative sample of individuals who have experienced significant and, often, extreme losses. That is essentially why I have included the words "other" in the subtitle of this book. Losses referred to in this book are primarily physical losses or, at least, diminished abilities to function physically prior to the onset of the losses. But look around you. Think or any individual you know or observe—a neighbor who has just lost his job, a relative who lost a wife because of divorce, or even an all-American boy once followed closely by the local newspaper for his outstanding athletic excellence who never made it to the pros. I bet O.J. Simpson knows about losses too. The plain and simple fact is that dealing with losses is part of everyone's life and successful living means successfully dealing with losses, whereas unsuccessful living is, quite simply, the opposite. Some losses happen to be premature, unpredictable, and quite overwhelming and traumatic. But it is commonly agreed upon by psychologists, social workers, and essentially any wise individual that the successful confrontation of a loss usually brings on something new—a crisis that creates that catalyst for change into new opportunities, new ideas, new perceptions, and greater enrichment mentally, physically, and spiritually. We have often heard the metaphor: When one door closes, another opens. I don't necessarily agree with that because doors do not open automatically. When a door is shut behind us, we need to go to the new door and initiate the process of opening it. Far too often we return to the old door and futilely try to open that one again. As well, this old door most likely fortified with so many locks, Houdini wouldn't be able to figure it out even if he had three years to solve it.

And in our achievement-oriented corporation-dominated country of America comprised of people whom Eric Fromm characterized as individuals with marketing personalities, there are serious ethical deficiencies as reflected in our legal, economic, and even, in my opinion, school systems which place a high value upon images and appearances rather than personal fulfillment and growth. My basic and, perhaps, oversimplified view is that people are not given the adequate preparation and training on how to accomplish this crucial life process: acquiring personal growth and satisfaction which essentially and simply is constructively dealing with loss. Losses mean dealing with something that is painful and troublesome. It also means transitions into new options which, in turn, lead to feelings of vulnerability, humility, and that dreadful sense that things are out of control, a real no-no for the image of the successful self-made individual who squandered somehow to the top in the survival of the fittest race.

As a clinical social worker practicing in psychotherapy for the past twenty years, as well as an individual who has experienced (notice I did not say suffered) what most likely the vast majority of people would describe as losses of magnificent proportions, I believe that I am in a unique position to write a book that not only portrays the constructive grieving process in dealing with losses, but offers action-oriented solutions towards positive change in the wake of loss. I am not only writing about losses experienced by 48,000,000 disabled Americans but about other disadvantaged groups such as minorities, victims of sexual and physical abuse, veterans of the Vietnam War and other catastrophic events, displaced housewives and other female groups, single parents, and others from the long list of the unfortunate subpopulation groups, a total number that has once been said to exceed three times that of America's total population. You can see that losses are the central issue since all it means to be a member of a disadvantaged group is to experi- · ence the loss of an advantage of the non-disadvantaged groups. Finally, considering the leftover "normal" population which, according to my balance sheet, would be a vast negative number since everyone seems to be able to fit into at least two types of disadvantaged groups, we would still have those inevitable and necessary losses throughout the "normal" life cycle, loss of a loved one, facing up to the loss of life itself, and so forth. Thus, this is virtually a book about losses, about changing and, ultimately, about growing; a book about the human experience that applies to us all whether we deny the reality of losses or accept them.

I truly believe that the basic root of the global problems that confront us here on this earth, including the threat to our environment as well as world peace, lies in the majority of people's inability to become personally empowered on a genuine level, that is, acquiring a greater sense of control and peace in one's life through changing and growing in the process of accepting and successfully confronting losses. The majority of us, including those in significant leadership positions in business and government, believe that peaceful living results from controlling external circumstances, ideas, behaviors or other people and, ultimately, other people themselves. The reason for this is that we need these other people to feel validated and worthy. Shifting from this external locus of control related to the outside world to a more internal locus of control, that is, depending on ourselves to make us feel good about ourselves, is in itself a major transition, a major loss to this typically end result of successful shifting from one stage to another in the usual or unusual life cycle. This is a major, dramatic and often traumatic shift which, for some people, occurs dramatically in one life stage (such as mid-life crisis we so often hear about) while yet for others it occurs catastrophically due to some uncontrollable, unavoidable change of cataclysmic proportions. Over and over again as a practicing psychotherapist, I have simply come to realize that my job in helping people who come to my office in a panic, is helping them to let go of trying to control things in the external world, or things out of control in their internal world, such as physical disability, and encourage them to focus their time and energy on things they can control, including the way they perceive themselves, making greater efforts to communicate better and be friendlier with other people, working harder on personal goals, and accepting responsibility for their lives rather than blaming other people and external circumstances. The implication of all of this is that losses, whether "normal" or traumatic, does not automatically convert to growth but often to regression and self-neglect (including mental illness). The difference between the former and the latter is the exercise of our free will, our awareness, and conscientiousness to seize these times of inevitable losses as possibilities and opportunities for growth. We must use our awareness and will to turn away from the door that has locked forever behind us and turn towards the new door—to open it, uncomfortable or vulnerable as we may feel, and frightening as it may be. In this book, I would like to give the reader the opportunity to see that, even in the most extreme external circumstances, a choice is still possible since it would be obvious in most of the circumstances described that a choice could have been made between retreating into social isolation or battling it out against the odds to find different and new ways to get our fundamental human needs met. But this book will also bring out, hopefully, another crucial aspect of growing through losses and that is the crucial role of positive support systems, simply meaning people helping others to get through their losses. In essence, I would like this book to be a sort of support system for those who are struggling with their own unique loss or set of losses.

The capacity to cope with losses and to move on with a life that is enriched with new ideas and possibilities does not depend on the type and severity of the loss itself, but perhaps even more so on the quality of support systems surrounding the individual at the anticipation and/or wake of the loss, whether they be friends, family, co-workers, or even professional counselors. The level of maturity at the time of the loss is significant as well, as one can easily imagine the significance of support systems when thinking about a ten-year-old child who has been told, for example, of the death of his parents in a tragic accident. Because of the complexities and multiple possibilities of these three variables: the loss itself, maturity level, and support systems, no loss experience is ever the same and each is highly idiosyncratic. There is no such thing as a "typical" loss, such as a "typical" divorce, a "typical" disability, or a "typical" death. For each member of the human race, the experience of loss is highly unique regardless of how the loss is classified. Thus, this book is an effort to create a new association of sorts with respect to the necessary pain of living, that is the pain of living a series of inevitable losses is not necessarily something to be avoided but rather, in a funny sort of way, welcomed so that new doors can be opened to a higher consciousness. It is only through loss or what others refer to as crisis that we must discard our old thought patterns, belief systems and behaviors in order to survive physically and psychologically from the loss. In my case, as much as I loathe my inability to see and, for the most part, hear, I welcome the strengths and resources I have acquired because of these limitations. I am quite certain that these strengths would not have developed without these limits or may have developed differently, in a weaker manner. This is not to romanticize my physical disabilities but to express a simple statement of reality in which growth is a series of losses which, when confronted truthfully and courageously, will create new possibilities and dimensions in living. That is what I wish to do with this book, to help you as a reader develop newer and broader dimensions in living by becoming more truthful and courageous in challenging your personal losses.

Chapter One

Grieving—Part of Everyone's Life in Growth or in Trauma, Like it or Not

"We live," Daddo said, "with a number of rooms inside of us. The best room is open to the family and friends and we show our finest face in it. Another room is more private, the bedroom, and very few are allowed in. There is another room we allow no one in...not even our wives and children, for it is a room of the most intimate thoughts we keep unshared. There is one more room, so hidden away that we don't even enter it ourselves. Within we lock all the mysteries we cannot solve and all the pains and sorrows we wish to forget. When Kilty died, it unlocked the last of these rooms inside Tomas Larkin and all the bitterness escaped."

Trinity by Leon Uris

Whenever anyone loses something that is important to him or her, it is going to hurt and be painful. It doesn't matter what it is. It can be a precious possession such as a toy, a diamond, or even an old beat

1

up, but meaningful, sweatshirt. It could be the loss of a loved one, or a job, or even a dream. Of course, when you lose a precious ability or bodily function such as the ability to see, hear, walk or think, this is only going to hurt a great deal and be very painful. As a matter of fact, psychologists, psychiatrists and social workers recognize that loss of physical function or chronic physical illness is, in professional jargon, an extreme psychosocial stressor. This simply means that such losses are very painful and hurt a great deal. But the important issue is that whenever we lose anything that is important to us, it is going to hurt and this pain is going to show itself in a variety of ways. Eventually, over time, this pain will subside or at least become manageable to the extent that we can function adequately in our daily lives or at least comparable to a level of functioning that was occurring before the loss happened. This painful process occurring after losing something that is important to us is usually referred to as a grieving or mourning process. The inevitability of hurting when we lose something that is important to us is the price that we pay for being human. In fact, if we do not hurt after such an occurrence, it is likely that there is something terribly wrong.

Because of the inevitability and humanness of the painful grieving process, the goal is to get through these feelings and not to avoid them in some way. If we try to avoid these painful feelings, whether it be by denying them or burying ourselves in compulsive activities, it will only come back to haunt us in some masqueraded, and most likely, exaggerated way. Thus, the first step in getting through these feelings is understanding them. To that end, we will outline them one by one. A word of caution: this book deals with taking action and focusing on solutions and not burying and immersing ourselves in the discussion of problems. Having power in our lives means taking action without denying the reality of the problem. An analogy might be helpful here. When our TV breaks, we take it to the repairman to be fixed. We don't have to understand all the dynamics of what the problem was in order for it to be fixed, nor do we deny the reality that the TV is broken. We simply look for solutions that work for us best in the context of our overall lives.

> "The line it is drawn,
> The curse it is cast,
> The slow one now will later be fast,
> As the one now present will later be past,
> The order is rapidly fading,
> And the first one now will later be last,
> For the times they are a changin'."
>> *The Times They Are A-Changin'* by Bob Dylan

> "...It seems that we have moments of turmoil in contrast to moments of peace in order to truly appreciate and understand that peace."
>> *Trinity* by Leon Uris

* * * * * *

The painful or bad feelings that occur when we become disabled are: 1) fear—this can range from mild nervousness to a lot of panic, bringing on feelings of shock and disbelief as well; 2) anger—this can range from mild annoyance to extreme rage; 3) confusion; 4) guilt—this can range from mild questioning of one's own actions to extreme feelings of self-incriminating blame; 5) humiliation and shame; 6) sadness—this can range from mild sadness to intense melancholy. To understand this one better, you might want to think how you felt when someone whom you didn't know very well passed on as opposed to someone to whom you were very close.

With respect to our disability, the intensity of these feelings, or simply how badly they hurt, depends on several things. First, the severity of the disability is a factor. Most people will probably agree that losing all of your sight is more severe than losing only a part of it, or becoming a quadriplegic is more severe, from a physical perspective, than a paraplegic. Or some people might believe that the loss of one hand is not as severe as losing your sight. A second variable is type of disability with respect to its onset. (A middle-aged man in perfectly good health suddenly and traumatically losing all of his vision as a result of a car accident might experience more grieving pain that a child who is born with cerebral palsy and who eventually becomes aware, in the midst of a loving, supportive family, that he or she cannot speak and think as well as others in the neighborhood.) The third variable is the functional aspect of the disability. In other words, how does a disability affect us in our ability to function in ways that we wish. An example might help best here as well. Pain over loss of sight might not be so great for a man who is able to continue his job as a counselor after losing his sight as compared to a man who will have to give up his job as a surgeon as a result of losing his sight.

Depending on these three variables mentioned above, the disabling condition can be so intensive and overwhelming that it is not possible to cope with it unless we use some types of strategies to block the pain. In psychological jargon, these strategies are often referred to as mechanisms of defense. Specifically, these defenses are denial, projection (blaming), overcompensations and rationalizing. Rather than confront the inevitable pain of the grieving process, we may tend to deny that it is painful, or that it even exists, or that there is nothing we can do about it because it is someone else's fault, or deny the reality of a physical limitation by proving to oneself and to others that anything can be accomplished despite the disability. It is human to experience the inevitable painful circumstances associated with the disability; it is equally human to use these mechanisms of defense from time to time during the grieving process of the disability, especially at the beginning or onset of the disability. These mechanisms of defense only become a problem when we get stuck in them or overuse one of them or a combination of them. For example, if we have the reality of our blindness or spinal

4

cord injury over a long period of time, we can lose touch with reality in other areas and become crazy. Furthermore, if we deny how we feel about our blindness or spinal cord injury over too long a period of time, it could affect our ability to feel in other areas as well. The important issue is that it is okay to use these defenses to get the painful feelings associated with the disability to a manageable level so that we can actually confront them and go through them. If we get stuck in these defenses, the defenses become ends in themselves, rather than means, and consequently we never get through the painful feelings. It is only when we get through the painful feelings can we come out on the other end in time so we can accept the disability and confront it. Remember, however, acceptance is only recognition of the reality of the disabling condition and in itself is ineffective, unless we confront the disability. Confronting the disability means we take action, positive action through the choice of activities that are within our range of control. We can accept the disability without confronting, but we cannot confront without accepting.

It is important to remember that the painful feelings of grieving are the price that we pay for being human. It is impossible to go through life without losing something important to us. Growing up through the stages of life, such as from childhood to adolescence, means that we lose old ways of seeing and behaving in the world. Think of the sadness you felt when you first learned there was really no Santa Claus. Growing up also means making choices; we must decide. The word decide, like suicide and homicide, has its roots in the meaning to kill one option in order that we can acquire another option. Thus, in a very real sense, the ability to grow and develop into powerful beings, and becoming all we can be, depends on our ability to cope with the pain of growing. I remember thinking to myself on many occasions that if I could cope with the pain of being disabled, I could cope with just about anything and therefore do anything that I wanted to do.

"I'm further off than I've ever been. This is what it's like to be dead. I guess this is what it's like to be a vegetable; you lose yourself in the fog. You don't move. They feed your body till it finally stops eating; then they burn it. It's not so bad. There's no pain."

One Flew Over the Cuckoo's Nest by Ken Kesey

"...But he won't let the pain blot out the humor, no more'n he'll let the humor blot out the pain."

One Flew Over the Cuckoo's Nest by Ken Kesey

I am going to outline the above mentioned painful feelings of grieving that I usually associated with a disability and present constructive versus destructive ways of coping with each. Please remember that it is okay to employ some of these destructive methods from time to time, especially at the onset of the disabling condition, or the awareness of the disabling condition, since the use of these destructive methods, usually involving defense mechanisms, only makes it more possible to manage and get through the pain, but we must do that, and that is, eventually to manage and get through the pain. Although the important issue is not whether we experience these feelings, but how we handle and deal with the feelings that we experience. Remember, feeling is part of living and signifies life, whereas nonfeeling signifies death or nonbeing. Feeling difficult feelings such as sadness and anger is just as much a part of being alive and living as is feeling excitement, joy and laughter.

Fear is a major painful state associated with grieving. Actually, fear, painful as it is, is the uncomfortable state of apprehension that we feel when we think we may encounter something painful or possibly annihilating.

Think of how all the times your disability brought on fear whether it was fear of meeting new people, or even getting back in touch with people you knew before you became disabled, or whether trying out new activities or activities you used to do before you were disabled. How scary was it for you to go back to the supermarket in which you used to always shop before you lost your ability to see or walk? What worries did you have that people you knew might come up and start talking to you and you would have trouble seeing them or answering their questions about your injury? The number of opportunities for fearful situations when you become disabled are, of course, limitless.

Destructive and often typical ways of dealing with these fears include denying the fact that you are afraid of new, even once familiar, opportunities and behaviorally supporting this denial by avoiding the possibility of contact with others, such as refusing to go to the supermarket, go jogging, go to school, etc. Eventually this denial leads to becoming more and more socially isolated, or at least restricting your activities and environment to only safe, and familiar places and deprive the opportunity for new activities and meeting new people. Or you may choose to continue to increase your activities at the same level prior to the onset of the disability but are untruthful to yourself and others about how you really feel about the disability, such as being scared. This untruthfulness will lead to shallow, brittle relationships with others, including your relationship with yourself. Dealing untruthfully with the discomfort of fear associated with the disability will lead to less rewarding, less intimate relationships with others and often pave the way for compulsive, overcompensating behaviors to prove to others and yourself that you're not afraid of a thing. As an extreme example, such a person may go to the top of the mountain and ski down the expert's slope even though she has never skied, even before the disability occurred.

The danger of restricting our thinking and behaviors to avoid the situations that bring on the uncomfortable sensation of fear is that our lives become increasingly meaningless and boring, typically leading to depression. Depression and/or anxiety (which usually is characterized by underlying depression) is the agonizing, numb sense of nonbeing and emptiness that often ensues when a particular mechanism of defense has been overused over an extended period of time. Depression does not result from a disability, but rather, results from a sensation that we can't do a damn thing about it.

Constructive ways of dealing with the fear are as follows:

Recognize and accept it. Again, recognize that it is just human to feel frightened when you lose an ability which once contributed to a sense of control by living in the world. In fact, one of the central issues about the loss of an ability is the loss of control, but acknowledging this and accepting this fear about possible loss of control will lay the groundwork for developing manageable strategies to help reacquire this sense of control.

Set a goal or goals. It doesn't matter what it is or to what domains of your life it pertains, such as work, education, community living, recreation, etc. What does matter is that it is important to you, it feels right and is meaningful. You are the only one that knows what that is, not your aunts, not your husband/wife, not your boss, not your best friend, not your minister or priest—only YOU. The goal may be major such as going to work or returning to school or minor (even a minor goal can be a subjectively big one) such as going to the supermarket by yourself, or calling a friend you have been avoiding for some time. The important thing is that the goal turns you on, makes you feel alive. Generally, a good method of goal selecting is to imagine that you can have anything in the world and think about what you would like and pretend that there are absolutely no problems in acquiring that goal, like making a wish. These wishes give you clues for directing your energy and behavior into goal setting strategies. Take time to select goals and, remember, it is best to work on one at a time to allow for full concentration, or if multiple goals are to be selected, you'll want to prioritize them in the order of their significance to you. Reading books or even consulting with professionals (such as psychologists or social workers specializing in career counseling) often help in the development of goals that are often critical, first steps in the achieving of these goals.

Make a commitment to these goals. Making commitments is one of the hardest things to do in life because it involves giving something up. It is easier to sit on the fence and not make a choice, keeping both possibilities open, rather than getting off the fence and making a choice, thus giving up the other possibility. But growing is not possible without making choices and choices have to be preceded by commitments. You may believe that the commitment to the goal you have selected might be too difficult since the goal might seem overwhelming, but, remember, you are going to approach these goals in manageable steps. A commitment does not mean that you are going to be trapped, but, rather, you are using everything within your power to accomplish the goal you have selected for yourself.

Break down the goal into small steps. For anyone in life, disabled or otherwise, it is unwise to get over the fear of water by jumping into the ocean. Rather, it makes more sense and is more manageable to expose yourself first to a glass of water, then a puddle, and then increasingly larger bodies of water. On a similar level, it makes sense for an alcoholic who might be too frightened to attend an AA meeting to first go and visit the site where the meeting is actually being held, and stand outside the door, eventually going inside. For a blind person desiring to return to a favorite restaurant, it might be wise to go to the restaurant on a day when it is closed with a friend, then to go at a time it is likely not to be busy, and ultimately to go alone on a typical business day. In psychological jargon, this approach of overcoming fear is usually referred to as "successive approximations."

Here is an example of a goal and the steps necessary to accomplish it. Following is a case of a 21-year-old man, a former truck driver, who acquired a spinal cord injury two years ago.

Goal: Obtaining a college degree.

Possible first objective: Gain admission to a school.

Steps in this process could include:

- Telephoning various colleges to obtain information about courses of study, tuition rates, locations, etc.
- Selecting a field of study or, at least, a provisional field of study.
- Telephoning representatives of colleges which seem interesting.
- Telephoning graduates of interesting schools.
- Meeting with representatives, graduates, or students of various colleges at their homes or at the college.
- Arranging formal interviews.
- Attending formal interviews, such as with an admission counselor or dean.
- Gathering more information about the schools from reading and meetings.
- Selecting schools.
- Applying to schools.
- Arranging to meet schools admission criteria such as taking SAT and arranging to have high school transcript sent to college, etc.

The important issue here is not actually what the steps are or the content of the steps, but, rather, that the steps are small, broken down and manageable. It is not necessary at the onset of establishing a goal that every single step be elucidated or charted out in order to accomplish the goal such as in this example of getting a degree, but once the process of setting steps toward a goal has begun, it is likely that that process will continue. Gaining mastery in small steps will give an increasing sense of confidence toward continuing the steps toward the completion of the goal. It may seem that the number of steps toward the accomplishment of the goal is infinitesimal and that's why commitment is so important. Many people often sabotage their own success by not carrying out goals that they have set for themselves. Another important issue is that we take pride in each small step that we accomplish, that is, accomplishing things that are in our control, but, at the same time, recognizing that these steps are a means and not goals in themselves.

Another important thing is that by breaking these goals into manageable steps, we are converting or getting ready to convert, potential energy into action. We want to change inaction into action. As a matter of fact, the focus is changing to new, positive behaviors toward our own self-fulfillment. Even in writing this book, I spent countless hours sitting around thinking about how such a good book could be written and how it would be useful for people with disabilities, but it was only after I sprang into action by turning on the dictating machine and speaking that I converted awareness into changed behavior. Breaking goals into small steps makes change more possible, feasible and enjoyable. It is fear that often inhibits the successful accomplishment of goals. The ultimate reality is that life cannot be lived without fear and that it is okay to be afraid but to go for your goals anyway. In fact, it is the fear itself that often makes the accomplishment of these goals exhilarating once they are achieved. But fear becomes more manageable and less of an obstacle when goals are broken down. Thus, when pursuing a goal-directed activity you may be more likely to say to yourself, "This is scary, but I'm going to do it anyway," rather than "This is too scary, I can't do this" or "I'm not afraid of this." Once again, fear is the uncomfortable response to the anticipation of possible painful states listed below rather than an integral part of the grieving process and for this reason will be discussed later in this book.

* * * * * *

Anger is usually the first painful emotion that hits us when we become confronted with a loss. When something important is taken away from us, it is not only appropriate, but healthy, to become angry about that. The emotion of anger about not being able to drive the car the way one used to is not different from the emotion of a child who is restricted from playing with his favorite toy because it is bedtime. The experience of anger is always valid, but its expression and meaning and its appropriateness depend on the source of the anger. It is one thing for a woman to become angry because her purse has been snatched; it is another thing for her to become angry because her next door neighbor did not voluntarily give her a Cadillac for which she never even asked. These examples are extreme for purposes of clarity, but in the former case, the source of the anger is based on reality, whereas, of course, in the latter case it is not. In both cases, the feeling of anger may be valid, since the feeling is experienced as anger, but how the anger is dealt with, perceived and expressed (verbally or behaviorally) will be two different situations. In the former case, if the lady goes to the police station and reports the purse snatching in a rage, her behavior would most likely be considered appropriate, whereas if she did the same thing because she did not get the Cadillac she fantasized about, her behavior would be considered very inappropriate, even bizarre, and could be grounds for involuntary psychiatric hospitalization.

In the case of a disability, when we lose something precious, such as sight, hearing or the ability to walk, it is appropriate that we would feel very angry, and even, at times, in a rage about this. But, care must be taken to see that this anger and rage are dealt with constructively, especially in a society such as ours which generally frowns upon the open expression of anger. When looking at the constructive and destructive manners in handling anger, think about the powerful energy anger has and how, if channeled constructively, it could serve as tremendous energy toward the pursuit of our goals. I remember once that I skied my best event in a downhill race on my second trial partly because I was so angry at myself for failing to properly care for my ski goggles in the first trial, a mistake that cost me precious seconds.

The *destructive use* of anger usually occurs when your anger is placed on something or someone that was not the source of the anger, or on something or someone on whom the anger is being taken out simply because you don't know what else to do with it, and that person or thing happens to be in close proximity. (This can involve displacing your anger about your blindness or inability to walk, or just the simple fact that you can't go to the supermarket the way you used to be able to without a friend or relative who may or may not be trying to assist you.) The inappropriate expression of this anger could include a wide range of behaviors such as arguing, yelling, or even passive withdrawal and distancing. The form of the anger does not necessarily take on a desire to resolve an injustice that you believe has been served against you by someone about whom you care and wish to maintain a relationship, but rather, is random, displaced effort of discharging an emotion which you feel you have no control over. This type of destructively expressed anger can not only lead to problems of broken friendships and relationships leading to increased isolation, but also increased isolation with ourselves because of anger that is turned in on ourselves and leads to depression. Often, the destructive expression of anger results from a sense of helplessness and is a last, desperate attempt for control before plunging into depression and despair. The idea of regaining control over our lives becomes hopelessly lost and undifferentiated, diffused anger is a last ditch effort to prevent a feeling of despair.

The root of expressing anger *constructively* is regaining a sense of control over our lives. You may eventually realize that there is no one to blame for the blindness, or that blaming someone whether it be ourselves or others, leads nowhere with respect to getting our sight back, and so attaching the anger to things or people you have no control over is going to lead nowhere. But if we attach the anger to achievable goals, such as those described above in the Fear section, it may serve as a tremendous source of energy. So, after acknowledging and accepting the anger that goes with the disability, it is useful to attach it to goal-directed behaviors that are within our range of control. For example, it may serve no useful purpose for a blind man to take out his anger on a family member since this could ultimately lead to separation, depression, etc., but it could be very useful to attach this anger toward a constructive goal such as the establishment of a self-help group or political group to lobby for the needs and rights of the disabled. In anger, as with all the other difficult feelings associated with grieving over a physical loss, it is especially important to keep a "watchful eye" over ourselves, monitoring and thinking through our anger. In psychological jargon we refer to this as an observant ego. Simply speaking, this means that we are watching ourselves very much in the same way we are watching and monitoring over a close friend or relative about whom we care deeply. This involves thinking through and literally could mean saying to ourselves such things as, "Okay, I feel really angry about this (loss of sight, loss of ability to read the newspaper like you used to, etc.), but if I take it out on my wife and yell at her for something I'm not really angry about such as not having a meal on time or her being on the phone too long with another friend, I'll alienate her and possibly, over time, lose her support. I would be better channeling my anger into making phone calls and inquiring about how to get the newspaper read onto audio tapes, lobbying for equal access to my city's major newspaper or even asking my wife assertively, but politely if she would mind reading the newspaper for me at a time that is convenient for her." This "thinking through" of anger delays immediate impulsive gratifications which are usually destructive and it leads toward more constructive and growth-enhancing solution. Looking at this a little philosophically and on a more grand, social scale, anger can be the useful force towards directing our society in a more humane positive direction away from impulsive, self-indulgent patterns which often lead to social corruption. Disabled individuals who have constructively challenged the awesome task of managing intense anger can serve as role models—not only role models for handling anger, but role models dealing with the inevitable suffering in life that goes along with growth.

A major loss is psychologically stressful and it interferes with our ability to mentally function as well as we could before the loss. It results in *confusion*, poor concentration, and other difficulties in thinking. Therefore, certain elements of mental functioning and thinking are going to be affected in a negative manner. This is only inevitable and part of the grieving process. It is natural, after a major loss to have less ability to concentrate, to remember things both on a short-term and long-term basis and more difficult to reason things out, and understand things on a logical basis the way we could before the loss. Confusion is another inevitable painful aspect of the grieving process. Again, understanding this as a fact itself helps us to deal with this.

A nonconstructive way of dealing with this confusion and other negative psychological states is to try to deny it or react to the confusion in a frustrated non-accepting manner. It is almost like having an internal dialogue as follows:

"I am confused (forgetting things, etc.) and I shouldn't be. Why can't I think clearly the way I used to?"

This reaction to the inevitable psychological state of confusion in the grieving process is a negative, self-depreciating manner which only leads to more stress and, of course, more confusion and other negative mental processes.

Constructive ways of dealing with the confusion and other mental difficulties are, after its acceptance, prioritizing and breaking activities into smaller more manageable steps. Understanding that the confusion will most likely dissipate after the grieving process is successfully resolved is also helpful. Specific strategies, such as note-taking or recording for forgetfulness, are more likely to be developed if these negative states are accepted. Constructive communication strategies which will be discussed more extensively in Chapter Four are also helpful in that we will more likely be able to get the help that we need.

Guilt is a critical, difficult component of the grieving process. Guilt associated with any loss is inevitable and inescapable. It is another price we have to pay for the freedom of choices and being human. A goal of successful grieving is not to try to avoid or eliminate guilt, but, again, to put it in its proper perspective and manage it. It is inevitable for someone who has lost the ability to walk because of a tragic car accident to continuously ask herself if the terrible accident could have been avoided if she had left home an hour earlier. The person who has lost his eyesight to diabetic retinopathy may besiege himself with the notion that he may have been able to preserve his eyesight longer if he had followed a more careful nutritional regimen. Guilt feelings may include feelings not only about the disability, but circumstances associated with the disability as well. A person born with a congenital disabling condition, such as cerebral palsy or retinitis pigmentosa, may believe there really wasn't anything she could have done differently to prevent the disabling condition, but is likely, at one time or another, to have guilt feelings about her rage over her blindness, or her questioning whether she really wants to live (suicidal thoughts), or could even invoke guilt-provoking thoughts such as being born disabled because of a predetermined and preordained affliction. Again, such thoughts, at least to some extent, are human and the idea is to put them in their proper perspective so that they will not interfere with our overall functioning and the pursuit of goals. And once again, this involves thinking through the feelings, using an "observant ego" (as mentioned above), so that the feelings become manageable. With this feeling, like the other feelings, we want to avoid the "vicious circle," that is, the guilt provoking thoughts trigger the uncomfortable feeling, which in turn increases the guilt provoking thoughts. In psychological jargon, we

16

often refer to this as "reality testing," which simply means that the uncomfortable feelings are disassociated so that we can think about the disability and all of its issues in an objective, truer fashion. Thus, a person coping effectively with the guilt associated with a disabling condition may make statements to herself and others to the effect of, "All right, I left the restaurant at 9:00 P.M. rather than 9:15 P.M., but I had no way of knowing that the other car that ran the red light would have been there. There is always a risk in living and chances are always taken, even foolish chances at times, and what am I going to do, sit in the house all the time worrying about who might be out in the streets? I wouldn't be able to live that way." Rather than, "I left the restaurant at 9:00 P.M., it's all my fault, I'm so stupid, if I had only waited fifteen more minutes that accident would never have happened." This type of internalized guilt is often an irrational way of trying to control what is an uncontrollable situation. The same is true for externalized guilt, or blaming, which is referred to as projection using psychological language. A helpful hint in dealing with this feeling, as well as the other feelings, is to pretend or imagine how you would respond to a close friend who is expressing overly remorseful, self-incriminating feelings of blame and guilt about her disability. It is unlikely you would say to someone about whom you cared that you agree with her, that she should have left the restaurant fifteen minutes later. It is more likely that you would help your good friend see the situation in a truer, more objective fashion. Why not treat yourself like your own best friend? Humor plays an important role here too, as with the other feelings—an ability to laugh at ourselves, at the irrationality of our feelings.

Humiliation and *shame* often refer to how we perceive ourselves in terms of our identity, and the feelings can range from mild embarrassment and awkwardness to outrageous shame and remorse. Again, the goal in dealing with these feelings in the constructive grieving process is accepting them, recognizing them and putting them in their proper perspective, using an "observant ego." Growing and maturing in life always involves taking on new risks and trying new things and, therefore, brings on the inevitability of awkwardness and clumsiness, leaving people with feelings of great vulnerability and exposure. Being confronted with a disability automatically means that you will be confronted with new challenges and, therefore, awkward situations. It can be safely said that the greater the number of embarrassing situations, the greater the growth and maturity. Personally, I have come to pride myself most on the fact that I have come to be quite comfortable and accepting of embarrassing situations. I expect them, accept them, and when they do occur, I remind myself that, although the situation is embarrassing, I can get through it. As a matter of fact, the more embarrassing situations I encounter the better I get at dealing with them. Many times, the embarrassment is exaggerated and amplified in our own minds because we are imagining what other people are thinking and saying about us when, in actuality, they are not, simply because certain behaviors are expected of people with disabilities. Thus, a blind person might think to himself how stupid he looks when he is looking off in space while talking to another person, but, in actuality, the person who is being spoken to does not necessarily think this is clumsy or awkward because this is what she expects from blind people. When I set a goal for myself such as skiing a steeper slope, and its steps include the use of different, weird looking movements or devices, I take pride in the fact that I can display them as comfortably as I do. This takes time, an observant ego, and patient dialogues with myself as if I were talking to my best friend who suffered a disabling accident or illness. What's going to be incredible is that, over time, you will discover that the successful recognition, confrontation, and positive actions taken through all of these difficult feelings will probably leave you feeling mentally stronger, and most likely even more mentally strong than you felt prior to your disability. The successful and repetitive challenging and confrontation of all these feelings are going to have a mental conditioning effect, the same way physical conditioning makes us feel physically stronger.

With sadness the key, again, is the recognition and acceptance of the feeling and putting it in the proper perspective. It is easy to confuse sadness with depression, but, basically, sadness is a feeling whereas depression is a nonfeeling. When we feel sad, we feel blue and pained but alive whereas, with depression, our senses are deadened. What often occurs, especially with sadness, but in all the other feelings with respect to disability, is that because things seem out of control when we become disabled, if we allow ourselves to experience a difficult feeling, that too will get out of control and perhaps destroy us. But, what we inevitably learn is that if we acknowledge, accept, and confront these feelings, they will not destroy us, but, in time, pass. In fact, if we bottle up these feelings, bury them underground in our unconscious through either repression or compulsive behaviors, they are likely to resurface in an explosive, more destructive manner. An interesting thing about sadness is that it can trigger happier feelings associated with the sad event, such as the good times that you used to have with your relative that just passed away. You can channelize these feelings into constructive behaviors that will not only help you come to terms with the loss but also can be instrumental in setting goals. It is important to remember that the source of the sadness, such as loss of loved one or loss of sight, cannot be replaced, and attempting to do so will lead only to destructive behaviors and make coming to terms with the loss even harder. In my clinical practice, I have often heard of parents who have lost a child and try to deal with their sadness by attempting to have another child and hoping the new child will fulfill all of the expectations of the deceased child.

The key issue with all of these feeling components of the grieving process—i.e. fear, anger, confusion, guilt, humiliation, sadness—is that they are inevitable, human qualities of the grief process and that we must get through them. It is only by getting through them, rather than avoiding them, that we can come out on the other side to accept the loss, in this case the disability. Only through acceptance of the disability can we come to confront it positively and develop personal empowerment to direct our lives to the maximum extent possible. A word of caution here, however, is that the goal is acceptance, not glorifying or romanticizing the disability; Merely accepting it so that we can move on with power building strategies. In order to get through the grief process, we must make the grief and its associated feelings manageable and the first step in managing grief is understanding it clearly and objectively. Then we must look for controllable variables. As mentioned earlier, part of the intensity of the grief response has to do with the disabling condition itself and that, in itself, is out of our control. If we acquired total blindness, there is nothing we can do to change that and thus it is out of our control. So to make our grief response manageable, we look for things that are within our range of control, and although the disability itself is beyond our control, the capability of understanding, that aspect of the disability is within our control. Through making a choice, we consciously understand that the intensity of the disability, in terms of its severity, type, and functional aspect, is not within our control. We are going to see an emerging theme not only in successful coping with the disability but in power building strategies as well that control is going to become a central issue, and that, for individuals with disabilities, control is a major issue and the ability to resolve that issue makes the essential difference between successful or unsuccessful adaptation. So while understanding the nature and intensity of the disability is the first major step in making the grief response manageable, the next major step is associated with psychosocial needs and our ability to fulfill them. Thus, the difference between a grief response being overwhelming or manageable is not only associated with the intensity of the loss, but with our ability to meet our physical and, perhaps more importantly, psychosocial needs. There is also a third factor we will be discussing in a later section relating to systems of support. Dealing effectively with these controllable variables—1) understanding the nature of the loss, 2) psychosocial needs and 3) support systems—make the difference. For example, the anger associated with grieving about blindness can be either manageable anger or out of control, full blown rage, depending on how we deal with these controllable variables.

Chapter Two

Psychosocial Needs—The Gusto in Living

"Nobody can tell exactly why he laughs; there's nothing funny going on. But it's not the way that Public Relations laugh, it's free and loud and it comes out of his wide grinning mouth and speaks in rings bigger and bigger or till it's lapping against the walls all over the world. Not like that fat Public Relations laugh. This sounds real. I realize all of a sudden it's the first laugh I've heard in years."
One Flew Over the Cuckoo's Nest by Ken Kesey

"The only thing wrong is submitting to tyranny. You have a right to inquire to anything you want."
Trinity by Leon Uris

A brief simplistic discussion is helpful here, and this applies to everyone—not just disabled individuals. It is obvious to most of us that every human being has physical needs. We must eat, have water, breathe, have shelter, and so forth. Without food, water, oxygen, etc., we simply cannot survive. Every human being also has psychological and social needs (psychosocial needs) and if these needs are not fulfilled, we cannot survive either simply because life has no meaning. For purposes of simplicity, we will categorize these psychosocial needs as the needs for 1) fun and enjoyment, 2) freedom, 3) self worth or feeling that in some way we count and contribute to the community and the world, and 4) love and belonging. It could perhaps be argued that there are additional psychosocial needs or that one of these four previously mentioned could be described in some other way. These four concepts are chosen for descriptive purposes and the underlying issue is that, unless these needs are fulfilled, life will have no meaning, or little meaning, depending to the degree that these needs are met. Simply speaking, unless we find enjoyable things to do, feel some degree of self-worth, are provided opportunities for freedom to explore the world, and have some sense of feeling like a significant part of a large unit, such as family or community, there would be no meaning in our lives and, therefore, most likely we would perish due to self-neglect.

Now here comes the important issue. Not only do we have physical and psychosocial needs, but the greater the ability to meet these needs independently determines our level of personal maturity and strength. It is essentially the ability to meet our psychosocial needs independently that determines whether we have empowerment building capabilities in our lives. Another word of caution, however, and that is the goal is not to try to meet these psychosocial needs independently, but, much more importantly, interdependently. We will discuss this concept later and it simply refers to the fact that no man is an island and can meet all of his needs in isolation. We must depend on other people and that is going to involve relationships. So the more mature our relationships and the better capabilities we have for communication, the more interdependently we are going to be able to meet our physical and psychosocial needs. For purposes of this book, we are going to be referring only to the psychosocial needs. The physical needs are obvious and, in my opinion, have been too much of a focus of attention with respect to rehabilitation and disabilities; that is, too much attention has been focused on disabled individuals meeting their physical needs in other ways with very little attention given to meeting their psychosocial needs.

Another important issue with respect to these psychosocial needs is that all of them must be met, not just some of them; therefore, they must be balanced out. This often involves a tricky juggling act and, in psychological jargon, involves flexibility and what psychologists and clinicians usually refer to as "ego strength." Ego strength, words I promise I won't use again, simply means a person's ability to make conscious choices to get all of his needs met so that he can function satisfactorily in the world and give his life quality and meaning. Perhaps the best way to describe the tricky nature of juggling these four psychosocial needs is to use an example. Many overemphasize the need for love and belonging and put too much energy into having a relationship and, in doing so, give up their need for freedoms by being overly demanding in their relationships and expecting to be demanded upon. Another example is too much conscious time and energy is put into our need for self-worth by plunging twenty-four hours a day into achievement-oriented activities such as education and work while neglecting possibilities of supporting and loving relationships. Thus, some people may value so highly the need for fun and thrills, living life in the "fast lane," and not disciplining themselves sufficiently to work on relationships or identity issues (the need for self-respect through successful vocational outcomes). The key issue here is that unless all of these needs are met in some balanced format, then needs neglect is going to occur and there will be a sense of "something missing" or emptiness in our lives. I am not implying that these needs have to be balanced out in a perfect ratio, but, generally, unless these needs are all adequately met, problems will result.

"...she flips a switch and the TV picture swirls back into the gray. Nothing is left on the screen but a little eye of light beading right down on McMurphy sitting there...And we're all sitting there lined up in front of that blanked-out TV set, watching the gray screen just like we could see the baseball game clear as day and she's ranting and screaming behind us. If somebody'd come in and take a look...they'd have thought the whole bunch was crazy as loons."

One Flew Over the Cuckoo's Nest by Ken Kesey

"The substitutions of pseudo-acts for original acts of thinking, feeling and willing leads eventually to the replacement of the original self by a pseudo-self. The original self is the self which is the originator of mental activities. The pseudo-self is only an agent who actually represents the role a person is supposed to play but he does so under the name of self."

Escape From Freedom by Erich Fromm

Another central issue with respect to psychosocial needs is *control* of getting these needs met, or whether we have external or internal locus of control in getting these needs met. This is where we start to get into dependency issues. The more we have internal locus of control in getting these needs met the more satisfactory our lives will be. If we depend too much on others to get our needs met, the locus of control will be external and, consequently, our lives will seem out of control, chaotic, and overwhelming. A little discussion of developmental theory will be helpful here. It is normal and appropriate for young children to be dependent on their parents to get their physical and psychosocial needs met. A young child must depend on his parents not only for food, but to feel good about himself, to have freedom, to have fun (where the parent provides him with games, toys and affectionate gestures) and, of course, love. The goal of growth and personality development is that eventually, over time, we will be able to meet these needs independently or, more accurately, inter dependently. Growth and maturity have nothing to do with what we acquire, such as wealth, good jobs, material things, but everything to do with our ability to meet our physical and psychosocial needs and acquire quality in our lives interdependently. Think about this. With whom would you rather identify: someone famous such as Janis Joplin, Jim Morrison, or Freddie Prinze—people who supposedly had "everything" in fame, money and possessions but who were also obviously unhappy and ended up taking their own lives—or a janitor whom you may have known once who didn't seem to have too much but always seemed to be always cheerful, projecting an image like his or her life was in control and truly satisfactory? Another way to look at it is think about all the things you have dreamed for or hoped to have either before your disability or now. Why is it that we want to have good jobs, wealth, and satisfactory relationships? We ultimately want these things because they provide changes in feeling states; we don't want money so we can simply hold the money in our hands and admire the green "C" notes, but we want money because it provides an opportunity to provide us with a pleasurable feeling state. Ultimately, everything we want in life is oriented toward a change in a feeling state and ultimately involves a change in feeling state with respect to these psychosocial needs mentioned. Thus, the greater control we have over our own emotions and the greater the control we have in managing our ability to meet these emotions through meeting these psychosocial needs, the greater the control we have over the quality of our lives.

Now I want you to imagine a continuum from 1 to 10, with 10 representing total and absolute fulfillment of the four basic psychosocial needs a 1 representing total and absolute unfulfillment of these needs. The greater we go into the direction of being able to control these needs, say from a 5 onward, the more pleasure-oriented and satisfactory our lives are going to become and thus, fewer, if any, psychosocial symptoms, or pain, will result from not getting these needs met. Conversely, the greater we go into the direction of not being able to control our ability to get these needs met, say from a 5 backwards toward 1, the more dissatisfactory and painful our lives will become.

Apply this continuum for each of the psychosocial needs and think about this. With respect to love and belonging, the greater that we move in the direction of fulfilling this need we will feel a sense of lovingness, whereas going in the opposite direction will bring on feelings of painful rejection and isolation. With respect to fun, the more we move in the direction of fun by getting that need met inter-dependently, we will feel enjoyment in our lives, whereas in the opposite direction we will move towards boredom. With respect to freedom, in the positive direction we move towards controlling our needs for freedom, exploration, adventure and curiosity, whereas in the opposite direction we move towards painful feelings of being trapped and restricted. And, of course, with respect to self worth, we move positively in the direction of feeling a sense of importance, or negatively in the direction of feeling inadequacy and shameful identity formation. Again, the important issue here is: what control do we have of getting our psychosocial needs met? The more we move in the direction of controlling the ability to meet these needs, the higher the quality of our lives; while the less control we feel over meeting these needs, our lives will become painful and stressful.

This is where defense mechanisms play a role. Whenever we move into the direction of a negative, painful one, that is, lose control over meeting our psychosocial needs, we are heading in the direction of a painful state. But, once again, to block that pain we may erect a defense mechanism, such as denial. For example, if we are headed in the painful direction of lacking quality relationships in our lives and toward feelings of rejection and isolation (which are painful), we may block this pain by denying to ourselves that we lack quality relationships in our lives, or by obsessively immersing ourselves in compulsive activities (fulfilling or, accurately overly fulfilling, the psychosocial need of self-worth), or by rationalizing the painful feeling by saying that people who have relationships focus on the wrong things of life. ALL these maneuvers block the pain of isolation.

Think about it. Think about the psychosocial need for self-worth. Consider an individual who is neglecting this need by failure to apply himself in becoming the most he possibly could become. Rather than moving into the painful direction of feelings of inadequacy and humiliation, he may deny to himself the pain that is associated with that either by repressing these thoughts into his unconscious, rationalizing that it's really not that important to "get a good job" or compulsively immersing himself in activities that do not promote growth in identities (including, possibly, criminal activities).

Now, another important idea must be discussed with respect to psychosocial needs. It is not only important to meet each of these needs adequately, but each need must be met in a variety of ways. If we choose only one method of meeting each need or one of the needs, we are likely to run into problems. I've always maintained as a psychotherapist, for example, that it is okay to eat once in a while for fun as long as eating is not the only way to have fun; otherwise we are likely to run into problems of overeating. Likewise, I have maintained that it is probably okay to have a drink of alcoholic beverage once in a while for fun, as long as drinking is not the only way to have fun. Similarly, with respect to love and belonging, if we choose only one person to meet this need, we are likely to be overly demanding of that person. Or, if the only way we can meet our needs for self-respect is through our jobs, we are likely to place too much value and emphasis on that and deprive ourselves of other the opportunities of feeling self-worth by contributing positively to our relationships. As you can see, the possibilities go on, but the important issue is you must meet each need in a variety of ways; otherwise our lives become undernourished, rigid, and eventually empty.

* * * * * * *

"I'm me dammit, I'm me! I'm not Kilty or Tomas...I'm me and I've got to live."

Trinity by Leon Uris

It is important here to comment briefly on the issue of *values*. The ability to which we are able to control, or have control, in meeting our psychosocial needs is dependent on the degree of our psychosocial, or personality, maturation, is associated with our values. Meeting psychosocial needs is a highly subjective, personalized mental and behavioral activity. Fun, for example, for one person might be something completely different for another person depending on their history, personal orientation and values. Someone living in Switzerland, for example, is perhaps more likely to think of the activity of skiing to be more fun than someone living in Florida. This is an extreme example only for purposes of clarity.

Basically, values are an orientation to life in which our perceptions and behaviors are, often unconsciously, directed as if we were looking through filtered lenses. You may have noticed before, when you donned a pair of rose-colored sunglasses, an immediate transition into a world with the reddish hue; however, after using these glasses over time, you lose awareness of the reddish hue. Values are quite connected with attitudes and usually develop throughout life, especially in the early, formative years as a result of learning experiences. The types of values are usually a system of beliefs and attitudes that connect in one way or another to the psychosocial needs described earlier. It can range from marketing or achievement values to political values to religious values to humanistic values.

Thus, with respect to the psychosocial need for self-worth, an individual oriented in a marketing value can meet this need by becoming a millionaire, or someone with a more humanistic value orientation can meet this need by volunteering in an antipoverty agency. What their values are, however, is far less important than the process of value acquisition and, generally speaking, the more flexible the ability to acquire a broader range of values, the greater the range of options and thus possibilities for psychosocial needs satisfaction. An individual rigidly oriented in one value without giving consideration and exploration to other values will suffer the distinct disadvantage of limiting his options and possibilities for needs satisfaction.

Now we come to a crucial point. Regardless of the psychosocial need to be fulfilled and the value orientation to that need, the basic motivating force in behavior lies in the pleasure-pain principle. Think about it. All human behavior is either directed to acquire pleasure or avoid pain; however, it is likely the avoidance of pain is a stronger motivational force than the acquisition of pleasure. This is simply a survival mechanism duly programmed, like computers, into our brain. Consider any decision you made since you woke up this morning or during the previous day. Consider anything you decided to do or decided not to do (perhaps more significant), and look at it closely to see the pleasure-pain connection. You may have decided to be on time for work this morning or on time to catch your bus, simply because the pain associated with the tardiness would have far outweighed the pleasure of delaying an extra fifteen minutes to watch more of your favorite TV show. Or, last evening, you may have decided to abandon your planned diet in order to acquire the pleasurable sensation of eating the ice cream. Or, conversely, you may have decided to stick to your diet simply by realizing the pleasure of losing weight—translated into pleasurable experiences of feeling lighter and more energetic—outweighed the pain of feeling heavy, overweight and fatigued. You may think about something you have been procrastinating for some time now, and looking at this closely can help you to realize that the pleasure of not doing the activity outweighed the pain of having to do it. Often the procrastinating behavior is terminated, for example, when a deadline approaches, in that the pain of failing to have conducted the activity—translated into painful experiences such as embarrassment and feelings of failure—far outweigh the pleasure of avoiding the task.

With respect to psychosocial needs satisfaction, it could be logically deduced that satisfying psychosocial needs such as the need for fun or love and intimacy will lead to pleasure, whereas not satisfying these needs will lead to pain. Unfortunately, however, this is not necessarily true. During developmental years and past life experiences, we can often come to make pleasurable or painful associations with events that are traditionally characterized as pleasurable or events traditionally characterized as painful. For example, it would seem logical that there would be a pleasurable association with fulfilling the need for love and belonging; however, if there has been a past experience in which a love relationship was painfully terminated, love can become easily associated to be painful, and thus relationships are something to be avoided. Freedom could become associated with isolation, self-worth could become associated with painful work, fun or exciting activities could be associated with painfully embarrassing social contact. It is basically these negative psychological associations with essential psychosocial needs that motivate people to the avoidance of fulfilling these needs and thus in a painful direction of needs depletion. This is essentially the principle.

It is basically this negative and painful association that inhibits us from basic psychosocial needs satisfaction, and similar to physical needs satisfaction, failure to fulfill our psychosocial needs could threaten our very existence.

Our psychosocial needs, or our emotional needs, are the motivating forces of our lives. You may want to consider the analogy of a sailboat in which the rudder, like our thinking minds, guide us in a goal directed manner, but the winds, like the emotions, are the power or the forces that push that boat towards its goal-directed destination. The rudder is useless without the wind (and of course, the wind without the rudder could create chaos). In order to feel powerful and truly alive in our lives, we must meet our psychosocial as well as our physical needs—all of the psychosocial needs and each of them in a variety of ways. This principle is basically very simple. The flexible fulfillment of these needs—all the them—in a variety of ways leads to a sense of potency and empowerment, a truly pleasurable sensation. Failure to meet these needs will result in a depressed state of feeling deadened nonbeing, and empty. But the trick is in order to reach pleasurable states of needs satisfaction, you must go through risk taking and painful experiences, whereas avoidance of these risk taking, painful experiences may seem initially pleasurable, but will lead ultimately to painful sensations of decay and nonbeing.

Now let's get back to the issue of disabilities. Before you acquired your disability, or became aware of your disability (in the situation of a congenital disability arising at birth), how effectively were you able to meet your own psychosocial needs independently, or, more accurately, interdependently? (Again, do not become confused by the concept of interdependence; it will be discussed later.) Let us compare two men, both thirty-five and blinded traumatically · and totally by a horrible car accident. For one man, let us call him Tom, he was relatively independent in meeting his psychosocial needs prior to the disabling situation. He took initiative and explored options in having fun, worked hard with determination and discipline to acquire a respectable vocation, respected and valued his freedom using it for his continued growth, and communicated intimately and honestly in his important relationships. For Tom, we can assume he has acquired a high degree of psychosocial maturation, or in psychological jargon "ego strength" and it does not relate so much to what he has acquired, but to his strength in his ability to meet his needs interdependently.

For the other man, we'll call him Mike, he basically lacked this ability to meet these needs independently and was quite dependent on others to meet them, or avoided meeting them altogether. Mike may depend on others, whether it be a parent, teacher or boss, to feel self-worth rather than feeling self-worth within himself. Again, he had a more external locus of control rather than an internal locus of control. Being too heavily dependent on others for his self-worth, he empowers people outside of him to meet his psychosocial needs for self-worth rather than empowering himself. This will not only lead to an oversensitization for strong needs for approval, but also overly exaggerated feelings of defeat and worthlessness if he is criticized. Likewise, with respect to the need for love and belonging, he may be overly dependent on a partner toward a state of being loved rather than having a more internal locus of control and being more conscientious of giving or providing love. Being overly dependent can lead Mike to sacrifice his needs for fun and freedom, or meet these needs in restricted, rigid manners without the risk of alienating a partner or significant on other whom he is too dependent for his needs for love and worthfulness.

Thus, after the trauma of blindness, it is likely that Tom, having prior experience and practice in meeting his needs interdependently, will have more ability in finding alternative methods of meeting his needs after the trauma. Generally, self-esteem has to do with confidence in one's ability to meet their needs independently. One who has relatively high self-esteem has a high degree of self-appraisal or self-awareness and is able to objectively consider and exercise options in meeting his physical and psychosocial needs independently. The greater the degree of self-esteem prior to the disabling condition, the greater the degree of ability to manage the pain of a grief response associated with a traumatic disability.

What makes the fulfillment of needs, physical and psychosocial, tricky is that doing so in a flexible, balanced manner during the process of growth is *stressful*. It is easy, for example, for a child to feel good about himself (self-worth) when a child who is legitimately dependent on his parents receives praise from his parents, but to acquire the sense of self-worth internally and independently (internal locus control), he must learn skills and capabilities through a formalized or informalized learning (educational) process. We all know that learning skills, especially skills that are unique and set us apart from others, are stressful. The same way as building strength in our physical bodies is stressful through hard exercise, developing our minds and psychosocial strength is stressful in a similar manner. It is helpful here to differentiate between good pain and bad pain. Have you ever noticed when you have exercised, you may have lifted too much weight or ran too fast or too long and rather than experiencing the gradual, stressful pain of strengthening, you felt a sharp, overly painful "bad" pain, perhaps even injuring yourself.

The same thing can happen with the psychosocial stress or pain during the process of growth and development. You can overload yourself with stress that is overwhelming, causing "bad" pain that is decompensating, or even injurious, causing regression and forcing you to function at a lower level, similar to the way a sprained ankle forces you to walk at a lower, clumsier level and often requiring a dependence on some type of crutch. Many times what happens is that we remember this negative, injurious experience and are often traumatized by it, therefore, avoiding altogether even the "good" pain of growth through manageable stressful conditioning.

Let us consider each need and also consider the state of mind and experience that occurs when we do not meet the need. If we do not meet the need for fun, we become bored. If we do not develop a sense of self-worth, we feel inadequate and worthless. If we do not develop love relationships or some sense of intimate belonging, we could become lonely. And if we do not experience the adventurous, exhilarating states of freedom and exploration, we feel trapped and confined. All of these negative states—loneliness, confinement, boredom, self-worthlessness—are obviously painful; so this creates a dilemma if we don't take on the challenge and stress of growth, we inevitably become pained because of the opposite conditions.

Let's look at these psychosocial needs from another angle. You might notice how they complement one another. For example, the need for freedom complements the need for love and belonging and, to an extent, also the needs for fun and self-worth. Likewise, the need for fun and enjoyment complements the need for self-worth and vice versa. How often have we heard the statement in our work or in society "business before pleasure"? As stated earlier, some of us can invest too much in the need for freedom at the expense of love and belonging and vice versa. Likewise, some of us can invest too much in the need for self-worth and work very hard at career and identity objectives at the expense of creating opportunities and taking time to have fun and vice versa.

Now consider this: when this overloading on one need begins to happen at the expense of another we usually acquire the opposite state of the neglected need. For example, if we put too much investment into fulfilling the need for freedom at the expense of the need for love and belonging, we are going to inevitably acquire the opposite state—love and belonging's polarized condition, namely loneliness and isolation. Contrarily, if we put too much investment in the need for love and belonging, we are likely to sacrifice our need for freedom and bring on its opposite state, namely, the feelings of entrapment, or engulfment or even claustrophobia.

With the above mentioned facts in mind, consider the essentialness of meeting our physical and psychosocial needs for survival in the world and to acquire a literal sense of being alive. Then, if we focus primarily on meeting our physical needs only at the expense of our psychosocial needs, we may survive biologically but feel no purpose and meaning in our lives and suffer psychosocially and, eventually, physically. People who do not care about their lives basically become self-neglectful, eventually self-destructive and possibly suicidal.

The problem with too many existing and traditional rehabilitation programs for people with disabilities is that they focus far too much on the physical needs only; that is, when there is a physical loss, they simply find a way to supplement that physical loss. For example, if we lose a foot by amputation, we recover it with a prosthesis, and that's that. Similarly, if we lose our vision, we recover that vision loss with new methods of mobility, reading, and activities of daily living (e.g., cooking, making your bed, shaving), and that's that. But we neglect to adequately and, when necessary, professionally deal with the psychological and social needs of that loss—a situation that is so psychosocially stressful, it, unfortunately, becomes tragic.

Here is a very important point. The ability to see, hear, walk, and so forth are not *ends* in themselves, rather, they are *means* for the fulfillment of physical and psychosocial survival. The ability to see, for example, does not fulfill our needs but allows us opportunities to see the food we desire in the supermarket or to cook this food. It also provides us with the ability to have eye contact with others and to find and transport ourselves to social situations we wish to attend. The important issue is that they are means for the fulfillment of needs and not ends in themselves.

Now consider this other very important point as well and see how it connects to everything we have previously discussed. Everything we wish to do in life—and I mean everything—has something to do with fulfilling these basic needs. Think about it. As discussed earlier we may say we want a million dollars, but it's not just to have a million greenbacks and gloat over them and feel them and rub them against our faces, of course, but this amount of money will provide us with more opportunity for freedom, self-worth, fun and even love and belonging. What would you do if you had a million bucks? Travel to Europe? What for? For fun and learning and possibly the opportunity to meet new people. Taking another item from your wish list, you may decide for yourself, regardless of the amount of money you might have, that you want to study to be a doctor, or a lawyer. What needs does this fulfill? For self-worth, freedom (when we acquire financial compensation as a lawyer) and possibly fun. The point is that any time we desire something in life, whether it be continuation of a previous desire or a new one, it is basically for a change in a feeling state associated with the psychosocial needs.

An equally important point is that these psychosocial needs are only complementary to one another, but also, each need has actually or potentially some of the other needs within its domain. For example, you may invest heavily in the need of self-worth by studying hard to become a professional, but within that investment you also can have fun doing it, meet new people, and find ways to take freedom and creativity in that endeavor. In other words, while we're investing primarily in this need for self-worth, we can find ways to meet the other needs, as well, during that investment period.

Now we get back to disability. But once again, remember this actually doesn't apply just to disabilities, but it applies to other types of losses as well, including *inevitable* losses throughout the life cycle, such as passage from the middle age years to the senior years. This is a rule of the universe: the goal of life is growth which is basically increasing your behaviors and activities that meet all of your physical and psychosocial needs in a flexible, balanced pattern. Of course, when we become blinded (or disabled in any other way), we may have lost one way to meet our needs, but now we must find alternative ways. The loss of sight may make getting to a social event more difficult, or having eye contact with another next to impossible, but these are only methods for meeting the needs for intimacy and belonging. The job is that now we are faced with a challenge of finding alternative methods for meeting the need for love and belonging, just as well as requiring alternative methods for meeting the other needs, namely fun, self-worth and freedom. Likewise, losing our ability to walk because of a spinal cord injury, we must find alternative methods of meeting our psychosocial needs, or, just as significantly, continuing the needs fulfillment process we previously acquired for fun, freedom, self-worth and intimacy.

* * * * * * *

"Come Mothers and Fathers throughout the land
And don't criticize what you don't understand;
Your sons and your daughters are beyond your
    command.
Your old road is rapidly aging.
Please get out of the new one if you can't lend a hand,

For the Times They are A-Changin'."
The Times They Are A-Changin' by Bob Dylan

That is how we begin to approach perhaps the central problem, not only with respect to disability, but to life itself and the essentialness of growth throughout the life cycle. We're approaching the central issue of *fear*. If growth and maturation, disabled or otherwise, possess the requirement of continually finding new ways to meet our needs in a flexible, balanced pattern, this means that we are going to have to continuously acquire new behaviors and activities, depending on the changes within ourselves and our social circumstances. An able-bodied adult—he may have acquired his needs for self-worth and fun by being a professional golfer, but eventually he is going to lose that capability because of aging—must find new ways of getting his needs met. Finding new behaviors and activities to meet our needs is going to require change, that is, something new, activities that are going to make us feel vulnerable and, admit it or not, scared. Think about the first time you tried anything new—riding a bike, swimming, learning to skate, going to school for the first time, beginning a new profession, starting a new job, the whole bit. Any activity and behavior in life has its beginning. Think about how you felt at first, awkward, clumsy, vulnerable, worried that other people might laugh at you and perhaps embarrassed. Interestingly, in starting anything new, we automatically bring on the polarized, negative conditions of a psychosocial need, namely, a sense of loneliness, inadequacy, feelings of being stifled, and perhaps even boredom. Confronting a new task means confronting these feelings and they bring on fear. Like any other psychosocial state or emotion, fear exists on a continuum, or a range. In other words, it can range from mild intimidation or nervousness to a full blown panic. But then, or course, the closer we get to the panic end of the continuum, the greater the likelihood of avoiding that new task. Basically, the central issue becomes; to what degree will fear get in the way or create road blocks in our growth in life, or our ability to develop new activities and behaviors that meet our physical and psychosocial needs? Is it mild to moderate fear or is it approaching the end of a full blown panic? This issue is a primary determinant in our ability to grow and to find new and increasing methods to meet our psychosocial needs in a flexible, balanced manner. Now, getting back to the grieving process of a loss, it is essentially this issue that determines whether we are going to get through the grieving process or make desperate and futile attempts to avoid it because of the panic that might be associated with it. One of the major things that determines whether the inevitable fear that is associated with growth in the life cycle is going to be a manageable fear or a full blown, out of control panic is not only the previous psychosocial strength, or practice, we have had in meeting our needs, but just as critical, if not more critical, the types of support systems we have, and this leads us to our next essential component—support systems.

* * * * * * *

"Conor there's a certain moment in each man's life when he becomes completely alive. Alive like no other time, when he lights the very sky with his vivacity. Of course some people..."

Trinity by Leon Uris

Before we get into a discussion of support systems, there is one more point with respect to psychosocial needs that is essential to highlight. We touched upon this point, which is about to be discussed briefly, when we spoke of values. It is essential that we amplify the issue to get a clear understanding of the essence of psychosocial needs. The essence of psychosocial needs is that they are highly and totally individualized. Depending on one's life experiences and other reasons not fully understood, the manner in which one expresses his need of fulfillment for love and belonging, self-worth, freedom and fun will be entirely different from one person to that of another. One person may fulfill her need for self-worth by striving for and becoming a doctor; whereas, another person may do this by becoming a garbage collector or even a welfare recipient. This happens because of learning experiences in which we make positive associations with different thoughts and behaviors.

The idea that some of us are "turned onto" some things and others are not, in part, can be traced to a biological source and perhaps be understood by taking a look at the brain and the nervous system. In order for society to survive and function as a whole, people must conform to certain rules of conduct and, to one degree or another, generalized expectations. We are all required to do things that really don't matter to us or we really don't want to do. For example, we may not want to stop at a red light, arrive to work on time, attend school and so forth. These socialized behaviors are, for the most part, governed by the cerebral cortex of the brain—that part controlling the central nervous system—which is connected with all voluntary behaviors whether it be thinking or moving. It is the central nervous system, comprising the cerebral cortex and the neuromuscular system, that allows us to appraise the world around us and its expectations upon us, and to make decisions based on these appraisals and expectations, and, ultimately, to make behaviors based on them. There is another part of the nervous system which is not voluntary, however, and is automatic which we simply call the autonomic nervous system. Let's simply call it ANS. The ANS is located in deeper parts of the brain and closer to the brain stem and controls smooth muscle tissue (as opposed to striated muscles of the arms, legs, neck, etc.) over which we usually have no control over. Musculature of the heart, lungs, blood vessels are examples and we all know that our heart beats automatically and our blood vessels dilate or constrict depending on the temperature around us as well as other psychosocial factors such as stress, anxiety and the like. The ANS also governs the activities of the endocrine or hormonal system, usually glandular organs which secrete hormones or other biochemicals which produce a wide variety of feelings, ranging from anger to joy and excitation. Individualized experiences of passion and joy, as well as negative feelings, are, in part, related to mental associations we make in the world around us and the types of biochemical responses in our brains and bodies to these associations. This is essentially why meaningful experiences, positive or negative, are highly individualized. In order to function most productively in life, we must find a way to balance the two activities of the brain and the nervous system, the central nervous system (CNS) and the ANS. Too much focus on society (CNS) leads us to overconforming, perhaps boring lives and, of course, too much focus on individualized needs without regard for society can lead to alienation and isolation. But, in goal setting with respect to the psychosocial needs we have been discussing, it is crucial to pay attention to your body, to see what types of responses you get when certain mental associations, or behavioral associations are made. It is often helpful to reflect back on your past and think about what you used to fantasize about or even daydream about to get clues as to the events in life that are meaningful to you. It is this fact, the fact of the ANS, that no one can give us answers for a meaningful life and the answers can only come from within ourselves. This is of crucial importance: of listening and paying attention to our own bodies and minds, looking for clues through the forms of mental and behavioral associations in which we become alive, or "turned on," with a sense of potency, fulfillment and meaningfulness. This is one of the essential tasks necessary in the goal setting and fulfillment of our psychosocial needs. Not even those closest to us—our lover, intimate one, family, significant group or society—can not tell us what is meaningful and important to us, and this leads us into a fuller discussion of systems of support. In fact, even a therapist, like myself cannot tell clients what their meaningful associations are, or what turns on their ANS. What a therapist can do is tell a client that he or she has control over his or her emotions and ANS; you don't necessarily have to make a million bucks or be famous for this to happen. Simply speaking, earning big bucks and acquiring fame is only another *method* for meeting psychosocial needs of self-worth, freedom, fun, and perhaps love and belonging. In fact, if being famous or a millionaire is the only way you can meet your psychosocial needs, you're surely headed for a lot of trouble. This is the difference between achieving to become happy versus, happily achieving. It's okay to set a goal to become a millionaire as long as fulfilling your need for self-worth is not dependent on being a millionaire, but if you find other, more controllable ways to meet your needs for self-worth, and strive toward becoming a millionaire, you will be happily achieving rather than achieving to be happy.

* * * * * * *

"The line it is drawn,
The curse it is cast,
The slow one now will later be fast,
As the present one now will later be past,
The order is rapidly fading,
And the first one now will later be last,
For the Times They Are A-Changin'."

The Times They Are A-Changin' by Bob Dylan

Finally we come to, finally, *systems of support*. By the way, I want to emphasize by repeating that we are studying and clarifying these various issues—grieving, psychosocial needs, and support systems—not for the purpose of dwelling on problems or analyzing them, but as a simple matter of clarification, for the sole and undisputable purpose of *change*. This fact will be clarified later. Now, back to systems of support. Remember how I talked about there really being no such thing as meeting your needs independently—your physical and psychosocial needs? I used the word *interdependently*. This is a very crucial distinction, and, as a matter of fact, I think the word independence provides the wrong meaning and leads a lot of people to problems. The old cliché is absolutely true. No man is an island. No one can survive in a vacuum. In order to survive, we have to depend on others and trust that they will meet certain expectations.

We may be able to earn money and get to the supermarket, but we are dependent on the truck drivers to deliver the food to the supermarket. We are also dependent on the store clerks, and other personnel to make that supermarket function. No one escapes this essential reality. Other examples, of course, are infinitesimal. We become more independent as we grow and learn to meet our own needs more autonomously, but we never become totally independent. Some of us are more independent in some areas than others are in those same areas. This has a lot to do with what skills we have acquired and what life experiences we have encountered. But we never become totally independent; we actually become more interdependent. We still must depend on others, even if to a lesser degree, in order to survive and meet our needs. And basically, we must depend on systems of support.

The essential variable that distinguishes dependence from a high degree of interdependence is communication. It is clear and effective communication that allows us to be dependent on others without violating others' needs and rights. If we communicate immaturely by withholding communication or, on the other end of the spectrum, by being demanding and insensitive to others' needs and rights, we are going to have problems in getting the essential help we need from our systems of support. On the other hand, if we communicate effectively, maturely and assertively (but nonthreateningly) we are more likely to get the help that we need from our systems of support and to acquire a higher degree of interdependence.

****

"But I remembered one thing: it wasn't me that started acting deaf; it was people who first started acting like I was too dumb to hear or see or say anything at all...*And even as far back as grade school I could remember people saying they didn't think I was listening, so they quit listening to the things I was saying.*"

One Flew Over the Cuckoo's Nest by Ken Kesey

Now, what are systems of support? Simply speaking, a support system is one or more individuals to help another individual to grow and to be able to meet their physical and psychosocial needs more interdependently. It can be a loved one, intimate partner, parents, family, formal or informal group and even society. Support systems actually provide three essential things: 1) guidance, 2) support, and 3) models of examples or role models. I talked earlier of the legitimacy of children being totally dependent on their parents to meet their needs, and, hopefully, becoming less and less dependent as they grow older. In this situation, the support system of the parents will operate more in a guidance capacity, not only providing behaviors and things that fulfill needs, but limits that are necessary for their own physical and psychosocial protection. As children grow older into adolescence or early adulthood, the role of the parents becomes more supportive since less guidance is required—at least it should be that way. All the while, whether in the guidance or supportive capacity, they are serving as role models; that is, they are not necessarily doing anything for the child, but just by example of who the parents are, they serve as a model for the child to test out his own behaviors and activities. Basically, the task of the support system is often a challenging and tricky one because we must provide a delicate balance of guidance and support, and often support means allowing space and freedom for the individual to test out her own reality and meaningfulness with respect to satisfying her own physical and psychosocial needs.

Perhaps an example is best to clarify this delicate balancing act that is required for successful support systems. Think of a mother teaching a young child to swim in a swimming pool. The child is seven years old. A healthy support system, or a support system that encourages growth and increased interdependence, is the mother that does not overly cling to the child nor provides too much freedom and space. If the child does not know how to swim at all, it might be better for the mother, at first, to stay closer to the child, showing the child exactly how to kick and stroke, not letting go of the child. But as the child becomes more experienced and demonstrates increasing stages of skills, the mother, inch by inch, can move further away from the child until eventually the child is able to swim on his own. But if you have a mother who never lets go of the child, the child will never learn to swim, and conversely, if you have a mother who simply just abandons her child to talk to neighbors at the edge of the pool, the child is likely to sink and perhaps drown. So a healthy support system is one that provides a delicate balance of guidance (including limit setting) and support (which includes the caring provision of freedom).

In order to successfully survive and cope most effectively with a disability, it is crucial that we nurture and maintain healthy systems of support. This means we must find them, cultivate them, and, most importantly, communicate with them. Now, back to *communication*. Communication is the crucial component in getting our psychosocial needs met after the disability and successfully resolving the grieving process. It is through effective communication that we ask, in a nonthreatening manner, for legitimate assistance from others, as well as provide ourselves with the opportunity to discharge our negative feelings of anger and frustration. If we are involved with a support system which truly cares and respects us, it will allow us the opportunity to discharge our feelings by expressing them to someone who *listens* with empathy, care and without patronizing judgmentalism. I cannot emphasize how important good communication is and how it will either make or break the ability to cope effectively with the disability. Asking for help is one of the major problems disabled people encounter, and how they go about it (whether asking for it or not asking for it) is a crucial denominator for successful disability coping for meeting psychosocial needs in getting through (rather than around or avoiding) the grieving process. In fact, this is certainly true for coping with all types of losses. In our achievement-oriented society, asking for help is often frowned upon, or looked upon as weakness and, this, perhaps, might be more so for men than women (although I haven't read any research about this).

Again, the crucial common denominator in successful, effective support systems in which the three roles of guidance, support and role modeling are carried out is communication. Let us return to the analogy of the mother and the child in the swimming pool. Let's consider the psychosocial needs that the child is fulfilling by learning how to swim independently without the assistance of mother or a life jacket. It certainly can meet the need for fun to learn how to swim. Likewise the need for self-worth and freedom can also be acquired to a degree, and perhaps even the need for belonging by learning an activity which can be done in groups. Now, what must go on between a mother and a child in order for the mother to be an effective system of support? The mother first must possess skills herself, that is knowing how to swim herself. And the mother must care for the child and his or her well-being (hopefully, unconditional caring). Then the mother must be able to have the time that she can structure to provide swimming lessons for her child so she can do so without interruption and with full concentration. Finally, the mother must communicate effectively with the child to deliver messages of guidance (instruction) and support (fear reduction, encouragement, etc.) to facilitate, as much as possible, the child's increasing ability to swim. However, an essential part of communication is listening—total listening—and in this case the mother must listen to the child for feedback for the child's inhibitions, anxiety, and indications of progress. Thus, the greater the ability for the child to communicate back to the parent, the greater the mother's ability to help. *In other words, communication is a two-way process.* The more the child trusts and feels cared for by the mother, the easier it is for him or her to communicate with the mother.

Now let's get back to the issue of disabilities. Visualize the mother/child model in the swimming pool, only this time imagine that the child is a fully grown disabled adult male, let's say about thirty-five years old. The same thing must go on for the mother (or any helper) to teach the adult how to swim, that is, providing good guidance and support, but now things are going to be a bit different. Everybody expects mothers to teach their children how to do things, say, for example swim. But now that this is a situation with a fully grown disabled adult, things are different, expectations are different, and there is more likelihood for feelings of discomfort and awkwardness.

Now, an important principle about communication is that, for *effective* communication, it is not only an intellectual task (good vocabulary, grammar skills, etc.), but also it is, more importantly, a function of psychosocial maturation. That is, the more we feel comfortable with ourselves and confident, the less worried we are about how we think other people see or perceive us, and, therefore, we communicate directly our own thoughts, wishes, opinions, ideas, etc. Conversely, if we are too dependent on others for the need for self-worth, we are more likely to communicate in a manner that is inhibited and restricted, saying things that we think that the other person wants to hear or not to hear. This type of communication is from a person with an external locus of control.

A second important principle of effective communication is the issue of responsibility. That is, we can do all the right things, 100 percent, to communicate effectively but we only participate 50 percent in the communication process. We do not have any control over how the other person communicates back to us or responds to our communications. Now, back to the mother and child in the swimming pool analogy, and, in this case, the disabled adult is substituted for the child. Whereas in the mother/child situation, the burden of responsibility for effective communication would be more upon the mother, since she has greater skills and maturity than the child, in the adult situation, the burden of communication is on both in order for the communication to become effective, that is, relatively relaxed, nonthreatening and comfortable in the guidance and support roles. Thus, in the situation of disabilities, it is primarily the disabled individual's responsibility to develop more effective communication patterns in order to more identify, cultivate, and maintain healthy support systems characterized by clear and optimal communication.

Chapter Three

The Dynamics of Change—
Risk Taking Towards Solutions,
What Separates Winners from Losers.

"You Chief, what about you?" He's standing over me in the mist. Why don't you leave me be? "Chief you're our last bet"...McMurphy's got hidden wires hooked to it (Chief's hand) lifting it slow, just to get me out of the fog and into the open, where I'm fair game. He's doing it, wires...No, that's not the truth, I lifted it myself."

One Flew Over the Cuckoo's Nest by Ken Kesey

"I dare nothing. I put nothing on the line. Even my passions are now frayed and pathetic. Once I dreamed I'd be a great man, Lowenstein. Now, the best I can hope for is that I can fight my way back to being a mediocre man."

"It sounds like a desperate life."

"No," I disagreed, "I think it sounds like an ordinary one."

Prince of Tides by Pat Conroy

[referring to ice climbing accident resulting in two amputations below the knee], "If I had to do it over again, I would...I felt very alive that day..."

Paul DiBello, International Ski Champ
Skiing, March 6, 1984

Now let's try to bring this all together. Let's say there are two individuals, both the same age, who suffer the exact same disability—total blindness. One is able to get through the grieving process and thus come out on the other end with a greater ability to confront the disability and live more independently than the other. Why? It can be safely assumed that the individual who is able to get through the grieving process has greater capacity for *change* because she had greater ability to meet his or her psychosocial needs prior to the onset of the disability and she was surrounded by healthier support systems which promote growth and independence. Notice, I said the word *change*. This is a crucial, pivotal point. To adjust to a loss is a process, one that can go either forward or backwards. In either situation, change is inevitable. In my profession as a psychotherapist, my goal with my clients is always basically the same thing; to help them change in a positive direction, to help them take better care of their own psychosocial (and physical, for that matter) needs interdependently. I facilitate the process of change. When a crisis with a major loss occurs, some type of change must occur to help to accommodate to the shock of the crisis. We could become depressed or more socially isolated. That is a change, even if a negative one, but this helps us to adjust to the shock of a loss. Or, we could adjust by developing new perceptions, attitudes, and behaviors to help us to continue to grow and to continue to meet our physical needs and psychosocial needs interdependently, and, of course, that is a change as well. That is, a positive change occurs. It is positive, basically, because we are getting on with the job of growing. The individual who's likely to change in the positive direction of getting through the painful process of grieving through a crisis such as a physical disability is the individual who's surrounded by healthy support systems which encourage growth and change as well as the one having prior experience in growing and changing (in a positive manner) prior to the disability.

It is the whole concept of change and taking positive action that this book is all about. We can talk about the way things were in the past—whether we had good success in becoming more independent in the past—until we're blue in the face but what really matters is what happens right now—this very moment. The future is not dependent on the past. Everybody has the capacity for change, regardless of whether you've had good practice at it before or not. It is just a matter of learning how to change in a positive manner. We have to learn how to change in a manner that would become more successful in meeting our physical and psychosocial needs, more interdependently and changing in a manner to help us identify and cultivate more effective support systems. This all depends on making a decision to take action NOW.

An important step in changing positively is understanding change and how it works. First of all, it is crucial to recognize that change is always stressful and painful. We cannot avoid pain in life—like it or not—simply because to grow is painful and to avoid growth eventually becomes painful. Remember when we were talking about the psychosocial needs? We can go in the stressful direction of growth or regress. Remember the need for self-worth? It is stressful to cultivate our identities by working hard, studying hard and the like. But likewise, if we do not do these things we will not increase our options to meet that need and will likely feel the pain of lack of self-worth (even if this pain is diminished or eliminated by defense mechanisms which will ultimately break down from one level or another). Somehow, especially in this society, we have come up with the idea that pain is bad, it is destructive and something to be avoided. Destructive pain that is overwhelming and indicative that our bodies and/or minds are breaking down is not good, but strengthening pain is good since it indicates to us that we are developing and maturing. This is not to imply the idea of becoming masochistic (which is usually making a positive association with an overwhelming, destructive type of pain), but simply to recognize and make a different, positive association with healthy pain that is a by-product of growth.

In my opinion, too many therapies focus on expanding awareness and self-awareness. That is, they focus on scrutinizing problems in the client's life, causes of problems, associations with problems, and, because of this, amplifying problems. In the same manner, it is not necessary to understand a problem in all of its detail just as we don't necessarily need to understand why our TV has broken before we bring it to the repairman. I do not think it is necessary to overly focus on and amplify problems. It is a good idea to have a basic understanding of problems, but it will be more helpful to focus on solutions and taking actions towards solutions. This is basically a process of changing a problem into a solution; that is, into solutions which will broaden your repertoire of opportunities for meeting your physical and psychosocial needs more interdependently. Too many people with disabilities have focused on all the problems that they have had, including psychosocial problems, by expounding on, with great (and often exaggerated) detail, their lack of support systems the lack of community resources and other opportunities for meeting physical and psychosocial needs, all of which creates an overwhelming, out of control situation. I propose, as I have tried to do in my own life, focusing on positive, realistic solutions and getting on track in a solution-directed manner.

* * * * * * *

"How does it feel
To be on your own,
With no direction known,
Like a complete unknown;
Like a Rollin' Stone..."

Like A Rollin' Stone, by Bob Dylan

Interestingly, I became fascinated with the whole process of change and what motivates people to change not only as a professional psychotherapist, but also as a skier. To change directions in skiing (to turn), we go through four basic stages—preparation, initiation, control, and completion. Each stage is unique and involves a different set of perceptions and behaviors. In preparation, as the word implies, we mentally and physically prepare to change. In initiation, we take action, spring our upper body into the direction of the turn we wish to go and release the edge on our downhill ski (the ski furthest down the hill). In control, we're beginning to edge on the new downhill ski (which was the uphill ski just the moment before) and come down on that new edge to prevent us from erratically sideslipping or losing our balance. In completion, we are maintaining in that position, and getting ready for the next preparation stage of the next turn. Now, what motivates skiers to want to turn (change)? First of all, if we don't we will probably injure ourselves by either skiing into the trees or falling badly down the hill. But more significantly on a psychosocial level it is to acquire a better sense of balance, more gracefulness, and eventually overall improvement in the meeting of psychosocial needs. This happens because we are having more fun by better skiing, increasing our sense of self-worth by realizing we're better skiers, acquiring more freedom with improved skiing and turning ability (allowing us to ski more difficult types of terrain), and even fulfilling a need for belonging by being with other skiers. The process of change in any area of life similarly involves these stages with an added stage of pre-preparation. Change usually involves 1) pre-preparation, 2) preparation, 3) initiation, 4) control, and 5) maintenance.

Perhaps the best way to describe these stages is through an example. Suppose someone wants to quit smoking cigarettes. In the pre-preparation stage, there will be little, if any, conflict or ambivalence. He doesn't want to quit smoking; there are a lot of good and pleasurable things about smoking so he has little or no desire to quit. He may make statements such as, "I don't see any reason to

55

have to give it up, I enjoy it, there may be a few problems with it, but it's worth it for me to smoke." In the preparation stage, there is more conflict and ambivalence about smoking; that is, the advantages and disadvantages are becoming more equal. Or, with respect to our earlier discussion, pain and pleasure, the pain and the pleasure are becoming equal. In the preparation stage statements are made such as: "I do enjoy smoking, but I am finding it to be a greater problem causing me shortness of breath. It's becoming more expensive, and few of my friends are smoking. I really am starting to consider quitting." In the initiation stage, the first step of action is taken after a decision is made because the situation is no longer in balance, that is, the disadvantages outweigh the benefits of smoking. Statements are made to the effect: "I've had it. I'm starting today and, definitely, I'm going to do something about it by developing a plan." In the control and maintenance phase, steps are taken to make sure that the change is maintained and preserved. This is usually accomplished through the involvement, commitment to and adherence to a plan that has been developed toward the goal. In our work with respect to disabilities, we are looking for ways to immediately prepare for change (preparation) and to initiate and continue change toward taking action. A change is directed toward successful problem-solving and finding ways to meet needs (physically and psychosocially) as well as to find solutions towards the development and strengthening of support systems. The continued successful completion of these tasks inevitably leads to the successful resolution of the grieving process (no matter how intensive the loss is).

* * * * * * *

On Reason and Passion:

"Your reason and your passion are the rudder and the sails of your seafaring soul. If either your sails or your rudder be broken, you can but toss and drift, or else be held at a standstill in mid-seas. For reason, ruling alone, is

56

a force confining; and passion unattended is a flame that burns to its own destruction. Therefore let your soul exalt your reason to the height of passion, that it may sing' And let it direct your passion with reason, that your passion may live through its own daily resurrection, and like the phoenix rise above its own ashes."

The Prophet by Kahlil Gibran

In order for changes to occur, new desired behavior must, in some way, be considered more pleasurable than the old behavior. This, or course, could be interpreted to mean the new behavior is to be considered less painful than the old behavior. In the pre-preparation stage described above, not changing is considered more pleasurable or less painful than changing. This state usually exists because defense mechanisms are in place. Let us consider a man who is afraid to go outside of his home because of his disability. He evaluates the advantages of exploring a community outside of his home in order to find increased and newer ways to meet his psychosocial needs versus the disadvantages of being vulnerable and anxious in this exploration of the community. By not leaving the home, he denies his opportunities and thus creates a greater likelihood of the negative states—loneliness, boredom, entrapment, and feelings of low self-worth. Considering the advantages with isolating himself, he may feel that he doesn't have to risk embarrassing and frustrating situations (such as physical barriers), as well as the usual healthy work and stress that is associated with growing by taking risks and confronting new challenges. The advantages of isolating himself could far outweigh the disadvantages especially when the defense mechanisms are in place, since he may be denying the reality of his psychosocial needs, or rationalizing to himself that he really doesn't have these needs, or even overcompensating in one area (such as self-worth by becoming an obsessive workaholic at an in-home job or study program). That is, isolation seems more advantageous, more pleasurable, and less painful than taking risks to go into the community. This condition could really exist if he is surrounded by a support system which includes, primarily, a family that takes responsibility for him by doing his shopping, making his meals, and even assisting him with activities of daily living in the home. But what happens, if by some sudden occurrence, the advantages-disadvantages balance becomes more equalized, let us say, for example, because his caretaker in the home perishes or moves away? He may have been unknowingly or unconsciously much more dependent on his caretaker (single or two parents) for his physical and psychosocial needs, and now sudden loss of these caretakers could immediately shift the advantage-disadvantage balance to a situation where isolation becomes more disadvantageous, or painful (less pleasurable) and change has to occur to reach a more pleasurable or less painful state. However, it does not require a crisis of this degree to shift the balance of advantage-disadvantage of an activity or activities, so a preparation for change and change will actually occur. There are other more immediate and easier ways to move through the pre-preparation stage into preparation and action by changing associations; that is, changing previous associations of activities that were previously considered painful into being more pleasurable activities. In the previous example of the man exploring the community, this would mean finding some way to make an association of the experience of social isolation more painful and exploration into the community more pleasurable. We often refer to these as *neuro-associations* and it is essentially these types of associations that can make us immediately ready for positive change and taking action NOW.

I believe a case example would be helpful here, a case I had recently in therapy. Mark (fictitious name) is a thirty-six year old man who suffered from a traumatic brain injury (TBI) around fifteen years ago. His disability left him with mild to moderate memory problems, mobility problems (moderate, walks with use of a cane), and moderate to severe speech problems (speaks pressured, garbled tones, but is easily understood). On a scale of one to ten, with ten indicating most severe, his disability would probably rank about a seven (with respect to the intensity of the grief associated with the loss of his functioning). He had adequate psychosocial maturation prior to his disabling trauma—attending high school with average grades and being nurtured in an intact family, with a father being continually employed in the post office and mother at home as housewife. On a scale of one to ten, with ten representing highest level of psychosocial development, he would probably rank between five and seven. He is surrounded by a limited, but intact support system of his family at the present time; his parents appearing to be supportive, but in this situation it is tricky because of many disguised, overprotective maneuvers by the parents which prevent Mark from taking more responsibility on his own. The strength of his support systems would probably rank around a four or five, with ten representing the healthiest type of support system. Also, his support systems are limited primarily to his family and perhaps one or two other close friends. So, overall, Mark is having quite a deal of difficulty with getting through the grieving process of an intensive traumatic episode of a TBI. Although he was successful in finding low paying, unskilled labor for the government, he is depressed about his disability, doesn't see much purpose in living (has expressed questions about whether he wants to live after his parents are no longer around), and is socially isolated with the exception of a weekly visit to a social club which Mark and his parents attend. He is quite dependent on his parents to meet his physical and psychosocial needs, he feels little control in his ability to meet basic needs himself. However, the pain of his psychosocial needs deprivation is shielded from himself by his defenses, through his denials and rationalizations of his feelings and behaviors and possibly his use of alcohol to excess to assist and amplify these defenses as well. In other words, the pain, or lack of pleasure of not meeting his basic physical and psychosocial needs more interdependently is shielded from himself through his defenses as well as an overprotective family system (his parents who tend to do everything for him). In therapy, we were able to isolate and identify one problem—his fear of making phone conversations in order to make legitimate requests and demands on the larger social system to assist him in meeting his needs. For example, he had difficulty using the telephone on one occasion to notify a vocational rehabilitation counselor to inform the counselor he did not wish his case to be closed after receiving a letter that was threatening to close his case. It was simply easier for him to have others, especially his parents make telephone calls for him. The reason for the anxiety, in using the telephone was his discomfort and embarrassment with the way his voice sounded over the telephone.

The advantage-disadvantage ratio was too far out of balance for Mark to want to change. That is, there were more advantages (less pain, greater pleasure) in not using the telephone and letting his parents make calls for him. This denial of the necessity to take responsibility for himself in order to become more independent, as well as his rationalizations that tasks that require the telephone are more effectively accomplished with his parents making calls since they could be more easily understood than himself, contributed to the sense that it was advantageous to be dependent on his parents to make phone calls for him. The advantages (lack of pain, increase in pleasure) of using the phone himself were far too few and nowhere near matched the disadvantages. One of his major rationalizations for avoiding the telephone was that he believed that he was less understood on the telephone than he was in face-to-face contact. In other words, if he were talking to the same person, that same person would have to ask him to repeat himself more times on the telephone than she would in a face to face conversation. My role as a therapist looks upon ways to shift the advantage-disadvantage ratio so that it is more equal to help Mark shift from the pre-preparation to the preparation and, possibly, action phase. I had to find ways in which Mark could make neuro-associations in which not using the telephone was painful and increased thinking and possible action towards using the telephone was more pleasurable.

A major issue in the pleasure-pain principle are the concepts of *impulsive gratification* versus *delay of immediate gratification*. A simple example will clarify here. Think about overeating. One of the dilemmas of being overweight is the immediacy of the pleasure by eating ice cream, but if we delay that pleasure we get the more long-term pleasure of being slim (not overweight), more energetic, and more vibrant, (not to mention the satisfaction of knowing you are healthier). The central issue is by delaying the immediate gratification of eating the ice cream, we will eventually get gratification from not being overweight. But we don't necessarily have to think of depriving ourselves from eating ice cream as being painful if we make immediate *neuro-associations* by thinking about how being in better shape provides us not only with greater physical health, but also more opportunities for meeting our psychosocial needs more interdependently. Being in better shape, we have more options for meeting our needs for fun, self-worth, freedom and relationships. Thus, we shift the pain of delaying immediate gratification into a neuro-association of immediate pleasure by making associations that staying in shape, feeling more vibrant and energetic is pleasurable, not painful.

Getting back to Mark, the first step taken in order to equalize the advantage-disadvantage balance to assist him from the pre-preparation stage to the preparation and action stages is to help him realize that not making telephone calls himself was more painful than pleasurable, and, similarly, having his parents make calls for him was more painful than pleasurable. This was done in a variety of ways. One was by amplifying the fact that calls on his behalf could only be made when his parents were around and they were not busy with other activities. Another maneuver was to amplify the fact that, when calls were made by his parents, messages could not be communicated in the same exact way Mark would wish to have them communicated. Perhaps, most importantly, was highly amplifying into Mark's level of awareness that his parents, being elderly, were probably not going to assist him after another year or so either because of their own incapacitation or demise. And with what he previously associated as being painful, new efforts were made to make similar activities as being pleasurable. For example, I offered a new meaning, a neuro-association, to his embarrassment of not being able to talk normally, and suggested that people with whom he would be communicating might see him in a positive light, rather than a negative one which he imagined. Imagine, I told him, how people will come to regard you as courageous for taking independent (or interdependent) steps in making calls for yourself despite your speech impairment. Also, I confronted the irrational belief that he is more misunderstood on the phone than in face-to-face conversation by arranging to have a staff member talk with him over the telephone, in a safe environment, and determining if that staff member, in fact, did have to ask Mark to repeat himself more times over the phone than she did face-to-face. So the goal was to get Mark into a preparation stage and action stage of making change by helping him to see, in small concrete steps, that not changing (becoming more interdependent in meeting his own needs) would be more painful than pleasurable, and this was accomplished.

* * * * * * *

What happens is that when the advantage-disadvantage ratio is equalized, the problem is recognized and felt, not buried by the defenses as it would be in the pre-preparation stage. When the problem is recognized and felt, there is greater likelihood that change and action will occur. And I believe that one of the most effective ways to shift from the preparation into the action stage, to shift from a position of readiness into immediate activity, is to focus on solutions, not problems. If we focus on, clarify, and amplify the problem, that is going to lead our consciousness into an awareness of the problem that is overwhelming and burdensome. If we focus on solutions or possible solutions to that problem, that will clarify and amplify solutions while minimizing a problem. It's as simple as that.

Sounds too simple, doesn't it, but think about it. Think about any problem you might have had in the past. If you've had a problem in your relationship with your mother (which may still be unresolved), you may think about analyzing that problem, amplifying it, thinking about when it began, how it began, the way in which it manifests itself and, in all, increasing and amplifying your awareness of the problem. But awareness does not lead to change. Awareness leads to awareness, and it is only how you use this awareness that facilitates the process of change. But if you begin focusing on solutions as to how to get along better with your mother, thinking of solutions within your range of control, you'll be focusing on, clarifying, and amplifying solutions, and increasing the likelihood of reaching solutions. You may think of ways to relate differently to your mother (rather than reasons why your mother does not get along with you), or new perceptions *(neuro-associations)* and behaviors to associate in your relationship with your mother. Think about cigarette smoking if you once were a smoker. You may have analyzed your problem with tobacco until you were blue in the face—thinking about how it began, why you began smoking, why you still smoke, etc. But when you began focusing on the solution, your consciousness shifted to amplify and clarify strategies that would eventually work and lead to permanent change. So back to Mark's case, the first task was helping him to see that there was a problem by balancing the advantage-disadvantage ratio (getting through the defenses to help him feel that not using the telephone was more painful than using the telephone, or his parents using the telephone was more painful than him using the telephone). Once this balance was shifted and equalized, the job was to move Mark into an action stage after recognizing the problem by helping him to focus on the solution to that problem.

Now, again, problem definition can be boiled down to, or broken down to, a change in emotional state that has something to do with either acquiring pleasure or avoiding pain. Avoiding pain is an emotion, a pleasurable sensation, and to get an idea of this you can think of the extreme example of how pleasurable it felt when the pain of a toothache or some other painful source terminated. With respect to pursuing and actualizing any activity that relates to any of our psychosocial needs, whether it be doing something for fun or something to feel better about ourselves, what we are really doing is finding a new way to acquire a change in emotional and feeling state, that is a change toward pleasure or avoiding pain. So if we identify a problem, such as a poor relationship with our spouse or partner (a negative situation in the love and belonging domain), what we really want to do is alleviate the pain and acquire pleasure by having an improved relationship with that person. Now comes the crucial point. The change in our mental state or emotional state does not depend on what happens "out there" in the world. That is, we do not have to depend on our partners for change, or other events in the world such as the economy, having a better job, having a million bucks, no matter what it is. We can change our feeling states regardless of what happens out there in the world. As a matter of fact, what happens out there in the world does not determine our feeling states although it may be influential. Believe it or not, we can control our feeling states by making positive neuro-associations with pleasurable states (including pain avoiding states) in the face of great adversity whether in the midst of massive criticisms from our loved ones, economic stress and, for our purposes, great frustrations associated with our disabilities. I learned this important point not only through my personal experiences, but it was also really hammered home to me during my skiing experiences. I noticed how well I did in a race was determined primarily by what type of physical and mental state I got myself in during the day and immediately prior to the race, especially when I got into the starting gate. A ski race, such as a steep, dangerous downhill course, can be a highly nerve-wracking condition, not only because of the hazards of the course, but also because of the competitiveness of the race. But despite the hazards, competitiveness and overall stress, I eventually realized that I still could control my physical and mental state. I had a choice of letting the stress of the race work on my brain and autonomic nervous system (ANS) so that my body felt tense, my breathing was rapid, my blood pulse was accelerated, and I began making anxiety-laden, nervous thought associations such as, "I'm scared to death. How am I going to get through this race?" or "Who's watching me? What if I look stupid, wipe out on an easy turn and make a fool out of myself?" I had a choice to get in those negative emotional and mental patterns, or to simply change my patterns by slowing down my breathing, breathing fully and easily to get relaxed and energized making positive *neuro-associations*. I would think about a beautiful run I had had previously or anything else positive like a favorite run I had taken once before and how it felt gliding beautifully and rhythmically down the mountain. Then I would begin to make positive mental neuro associations, usually energetic, enthusiastic ones such as, "I'm really excited about this race. I'm looking forward to it and I'm going to give it all I have and do the very best I can and really enjoy it." As a matter of fact, one particularly effective training drill that we used to conduct in Colorado was when the instructor would have us take a run down a slope, and for the first half of the run we had to, on a scale of one to five where a one was not going for it at all and five was going all out for it with a spectacular run, notice the difference in our feeling state when we were skiing at a one (not going for it, holding back, etc.) versus a five (going all out for it, giving it all you've got). We were asked to notice the differences in our bodies and our mental states and, most importantly, we were forced to recognize and to be made more aware of how we had control over our physical and mental states, that we can exert a change from inside. We learned that controlling our mental and physical states was a greater factor than anything else, including bad weather, the steepness of the slope, or snow conditions.

Let's get back to Mark's situation with his anxiety over using the telephone. At first his problem was unclear since his defenses were working and he didn't feel the need to use the phone, but when these defenses were broken through by having him look at what it would be like if his parents weren't around, then he came to realize more that there was a problem. Now that he is more positioned to solve the problem, that is, using the telephone to increase his range of options for solving his problems associated with his psychosocial needs, he has to change his state in terms of his association with the telephone. Rather than seething and behaving in a negative physical and mental state on his view of the telephone and using it, feeling anxious and nervous about it, worrying about how other people were going to see him and what kinds of opinions they might make about him, thus getting all tense, anxious and the like, he could now make new associations by breaking that negative pattern and changing his physical and mental state positively. He could begin to be aware that he has control over his physical and mental state regardless of the adversity he faces out there in the world, focusing on his physical state by more relaxed breathing, getting his entire body to relax and feel more energetic, and mentally preparing himself for a positive experience with the challenge. Rather than making negative statements such as, "I'm afraid to use the telephone, people get frustrated with me and always have to ask me to repeat myself," he can say, "This is a challenge. It might take a few extra minutes or even a lot of extra minutes, but just think, by using this phone I have more control of my situation. I can make calls on my own to see what is playing at the movies, what books are available at the library, and when my appointment is supposed to be with the doctor."

* * * * * * *

"And then the pain summoned me. It came like a pillar of fire behind my eyes. It struck suddenly and hard. In the perfect stillness, I shut my eyes and lay in the darkness and made a vow to change my life."

Prince of Tides by Pat Conroy

Consider your physical state and your ability to change it. Anything you'd like to have more of in your life (pleasure), or less of (pain), whether it be a great relationship, financial success, a vacation in Hawaii or the Alps, it is basically to bring a change in the way you feel to a pleasurable state, that is, change in the way you feel in your body and your nervous system. Think about when you are feeling sad, anxious, or depressed—all of these being negative, painful states. What's happening with your body? When you're anxious and tense your breathing is shallow and rapid, your hands may feel cold and clammy, your whole body feels wired up like a spring that has been wound up too tight. Or take depression. Remember when you felt depressed, your breathing was shallow, your body felt almost dead, no energy, downcast eyes, facial and jaw muscles felt weathered and saggy. When we get into a negative physical state because of the negative mental state, we can change that state. It is impossible to be simultaneously depressed, and breathe energetically, force a smile, and walk rapidly around the house or around the block. Try it for a simple exercise. Try being in a mental state of depression or anxiety, but having your body operate as if it were physically alive and energetic, by breathing in fully, moving vigorously, standing tall and lifting your facial muscles with a smile. It will not be possible to remain in a depressed or anxious state.

This is making a positive *empowerment* movement of changing our physical states even in the face of adversity. Good athletes do this in the face of their greatest competitive stress, as well as other successful people in all walks of life—in business, community service, and public service.

The reason for this goes back to our discussion of the autonomic nervous system (ANS) as well as the central nervous system. In the face of stress and negative (painful) situations, our ANS goes into operation; specifically, the sympathetic nervous system which contributes to rapid breathing, excessive perspiration, tightened facial muscles, increased blood pressure through constricted capillaries, etc. But, contrary to most people's understanding we can change these involuntary reflexes to voluntary activities. We can relax and make our breathing slow full and vibrant again. We can relax our facial muscles, and even slow down our heart rate simply by visualizing the process of body relaxation then it (rather than the stressful event). This is all within our range of control, and thus, it is not our critical partner that makes us all tense and nervous, but it is how we respond to his criticism. You can respond by getting tense and nervous or you can respond by willing yourself to relax and get into a positive physical state.

This is why role modeling is important—finding out what others who are successful do to change their physical and mental states in the face of adversity and stress so that problem-solving and achieving become pleasurable rather than painful. Again, the difference between happily achieving versus achieving to be happy. If role models aren't readily available, books can be read about successful people, learning about how they think and feel, how they focus their bodies and minds. Abraham Maslow was a psychologist who pioneered this growth-oriented trend. Rather than focus on psychopathology, he focused on self-actualized people. Voice is another manifestation of our physical state. When we are tense or depressed, our voices are somber and lack in energy; whereas, when we are upbeat and positive (positive neuro-associations), our voices are enthusiastic and rich in timbre. Incidentally, this principle accounts for the high popularity of drugs, including alcohol and tobacco. People take drugs to immediately and readily achieve pleasurable states, but drugs simply trick our biochemistry into positive feelings so that we feel "up" and pleasurable. In fact, one of the pleasurable aspects of smoking is the way it changes our breathing as well as the impact of the nicotine. Basically, drugs are used for immediate changes into pleasurable (physical and mental) states, but of course, over time drugs bring on more pain because of addictions, psychological and social problems, as well as medical problems. It was distressing for me to discover during my work with the disabled that included substance abuse research that the rate of substance abuse among the disabled was two to six times greater than the general population. Drugs may be effective in helping with the physical and emotional pain associated with a disability, but over time there will be more pain than at the onset prior to beginning the use of drugs. In other words, a person with arthritis may use legal or prescription drugs to help with the pain of the arthritis, but in time, because of the addictive quality of the drug, the overall pain will worsen. The essential point here is that it is possible to change our physical and mental state without the use of drugs. Humor is another way to change our physical state, a tense negative one into a joyful positive one. We can be in the midst of an angry, frustrated mood with negative *neuro-associations* in a strong negative pattern, but immediately and thoroughly disrupt it by changing it into a humorous situation. I can't tell you the thousands of times in the midst of my own adversity and struggles where I would snap out of my misery by shifting my mental focus and looking at even difficult situations with humor and humility. Doing this would make my body feel lighter, more joyful, and positive.

Chapter Four

Belief Systems—Our Ideas Which Decide Whether We Make It or Break It

"My parents had succeeded in making me a stranger to myself...I allowed them to knead and shape me into the smooth lineaments of their nonpareil child. I adhered to the measurements of their vision...They succeeded in not only making me normal but also in making me dull."

Prince of Tides by Pat Conroy

"Parnell gives Conor a copy of *The Rights of Man* by an American, Thomas Paine, and says, 'it has some very important ideas you ought to know about.' He goes on, 'That's one of our greatest problems here in Ireland. We've felt the nobodies for too long. You're very much some-body, Conor Larkin...do you understand me lad?' 'Aye, I do,' he said."

Trinity by Leon Uris

The goal of all therapies, not only rational-emotive, is to assign a new or a changed meaning to old experiences which highly discourage individual growth and maturation. It is highly likely, almost

71

guaranteed actually, that an individual who has not matured suffi-ciently to meet his own physical and psychosocial needs indepen-dently (interdependently) will assign much more threatening and fearful meaning to circumstances and events that occur outside of him. An individual who has not matured sufficiently, has not devel-oped a sufficient sense of power within herself, assigns a much more unrealistic (irrational, at times) sense of power to people and cir-cumstances in his or her world. It is a very common statement for me to make during a "breakthrough" in therapy, "Look, it is under-standable you are highly threatened because your parents did not show interest in you when you were a child. Being a child, you de-pended on them for your needs of self-worth. But now you're an adult, and their lack of interest in your desire to open up your own business does not have to be so threatening simply because parents realistically do not hold the power you subjectively feel award them. It is time you start becoming your own parent, making and respect-ing your own decisions, giving your own self more power." In other words, we are assigning a different meaning to the parents behavior of lack of interest and indifference, a new meaning that is associated with the individual's increasing strength and personal maturation (interdependence). We all have the power to embrace our basic hu-man entitlement, that is to empower ourselves. We do not do this by a false, illusory sense of self-inflated grandiosity (which is basically a shield for our real feelings of powerlessness), but simply by a genu-ine and deep reverence for accepting who and what we are. Why is it that, given a group of people facing the same adversities, some respond to the challenge and live their lives full of vitality and suc-cess, and others plummet to lives of struggles and near despera-tion? The answer is that the successful people give positive meaning to the world around them, primarily because they have a greater sense of internal control managing their own physical and mental states, regardless of how ugly life and the world can be at times.

Well, we don't want to get too philosophical, but a brief look at existential philosophy may be helpful here. One of man's basic existential fears is his aloneness, the inevitability of death. Some people respond to this existential truth by assigning negative meanings to these facts and living lives fearing aloneness and death, submerging themselves in overconformity, even denying these realities. However, others assign these truths with positive meanings, simply because they are human realities and deal with these truths living life to the fullest, enriching their relationships, living through a genuine sense of personal empowerment while respecting the power of the others loves, and so forth. Viktor Frankle, M.D., a famous European psychoanalyst and important existentialist who withstood confinement in a Nazi concentration camp, once said, suffering ceases to be suffering when we give meaning to the suffering. Rather than just give up and perish in the concentration camp, Frankle made a decision to assign new meaning to his confinement experiences. Not only would it strengthen his resolve to live despite the testing circumstances, but he would live to make a solid contribution in the future never to let these types of atrocities occur again.

By growing to become more independent (interdependent), we are not only strengthening the ability to assign new meanings to previous and current experiences, but we are also strengthening the ability to assign new meanings to circumstances in a flexible pattern. This principle, of course, is very much applicable to the issue of disability. We cannot change the trauma of the disability, or the severity of the trauma, but we can change the meaning assigned to it. We are changing meanings. We are not denying reality, for example, by glorifying or romanticizing a disability, but rather, we are looking at it from a strengthened, rather than a weakened, perspective. We cannot change the meaning of a word, a word describes an experience. But we can change the meaning of an experience. I remember very consciously and vividly making decisions that I was going to turn my disabilities into positive experiences, turn my weaknesses into strengths by accepting and even welcoming the challenge and use it as an impetus and catalyst for my own growth. I also saw it as a way to increase my own sensitivity for the struggles of others in their own growth, their own inevitable pain and suffering (inevitabilities throughout the life cycle). Thus, if I were faced with an obstacle or barrier such as a critical individual who intentionally or unintentionally patronized me or made efforts to embarrass me, I would respond to this by giving new, strengthened meaning to the situation by telling myself, "Look, the guy's trying to put me down, but I am not dependent on him for my self-worth and self-respect. I can handle this, due to my own sense of self-worth, and can even look at him objectively and feel some compassion for him since he is obviously not terribly empowered himself and is easily threatened by others." People who have grown and matured sufficiently are dependent on themselves for the satisfaction of their own needs, physically and psychosocially, and thus, having a greater internal locus of control, do not require validation from the external world and people within it. Thus, they are more objectively able to appraise the world and see it for what it is, not for what they need it to be (in order to be validated).

There is a beautiful passage in Leon Uris's book *Trinity*, in which Daddo Friel, a blinded wise old man describes to the young Conor Larkin (the book's hero) that the personality was like rooms in a house. There were some rooms where we let everyone in (most likely the living room), some rooms where we let only a few in (that's probably the kitchen), other rooms which we share with our most intimate partner (most likely the bedroom), some rooms we go in alone (perhaps the bathroom), and there is also a room we don't even go into (perhaps the cellar or darkened old closets) of course, representing the unconscious, we store things there we don't want to deal with or try to forget. A healthy personality is one in which there is a flexible balance of "people" we allow into each room. Perhaps there are many people in the living room, and five to ten people dining with us and one intimate sharing our bedroom. But, if we do not have a sufficient degree of power within ourselves and depend too much on others to meet our needs, people are likely to become threatening, and, therefore, these relationships have more negative meanings, and we are likely to have too many people in the living room, too many spooks and ghosts in the cellar, with not enough warmth in the kitchen, intimacy in the bedroom and privacy in the bathroom. We give new meaning to relationships with ourselves and others when we grow and empower ourselves. Pain and suffering is not seen in an overwhelmingly negative but rather a manageable, necessary and positive sense which contributes to our strength and growth. Simply speaking, we can come to see pain and even suffering as a good thing. We can give it a new meaning; that is, when we struggle and actualize even in the midst of pain to grow to meet our needs interdependently we can see these things as positive. Thus, we can assign new positive meaning to things like the pain of deprivation in dieting or quitting tobacco usage just the same way we can see pain in struggling with our disabilities, or limitations as positive. We can make a new neuro-association of a positive, vibrant fact of life which pain is. I think it is important to remember that the ability to be alive means the ability to feel, and that means feeling pain as well as feeling joy. The negative situation is nonfeeling which is emptiness and depression, two concepts to which we can legitimately apply negative meanings. In other words, it is healthy to feel pain while it is not healthy to experience depression.

* * * * * * *

"She should write about what won't hurt her, what won't draw out the dogs."

"She has to write about them Luke. That's where the poetry comes from. Without them there's no poetry."

Prince of Tides by Pat Conroy

Thus, we have the ability, through our step-by-step growth in meeting our physical and psychosocial needs as well as cultivating our support systems—of reframing new meaning to activities through the pain of growth. I call this shift in mental focusing, this very real and powerful change, *empowerment reframing*. This changes our perspective on the way we evaluate and appraise our goals and solutions in life. Think of it diagrammatically. Imagine a couple, comprising of an individual and either a partner or group of people who compose a significant support system. Diagrammatically represent the individual with a circle and put a small "p" inside standing for little power; whereas a second circle is represented with a capital "P" inside standing for a disproportionate amount of power given to that partner or group of people. Perceiving the "significant others" with too much power, the individual will behave and respond in either timid, fearful ways or overcompensatory grandiose manners. However, if the individual is represented with a capital "P" inside the circle, the individual is empowered relating genuinely, assertively, and cooperatively with others respecting their needs as well as his own. Basically what this capital "P" for power (empowerment) represents is an internal locus of control being able to evaluate the world objectively and meet his needs interdependently. Consider the need for self-worth in the situation of the powerless individual (represented by the small "p"), the self-worth would be dependent on the partner or group of people and would fluctuate widely depending on the whims and strengths of those other people. An analogy to this is that the regulator for self-worth is like a home thermostat. When this thermostat is deep within the individual (internal locus of control), self-worth does not depend on others, similar to when a thermostat is placed in a central hallway. Conversely, people who give too much power to those in the outside world (external locus of control) are like home thermostats which are placed too close to the window.

Now I believe this empowerment reframing, this positive shifting in mental focus, serves as the basis for enabling us to shift all of our perceptions, images, thoughts, and behavior into a positive pattern, a pattern of empowerment, represented by capital "P" in which the locus of control is within us (internal) and basically enables us to do just about anything we want to do. The beauty of all this is that it doesn't matter what our past is, how disabled we are, or what the limits are. What matters is how we mentally refocus to an empowerment reframing to take control of our situation in a positive and solution-focused manner. As a college student in the late '60s, I always loved the rock opera *Tommy*, by The Who. The opera, rich in its auditory and visual imagery, was highly symbolic and some people wondered if I identified with Tommy, being visually and hearing impaired myself, which could be partly true, but the bigger message was, of course, the shift in power. Despite Tommy's blindness and deafness, he was able to "smash the mirror," a symbolic reference to ending the giving of too much power to others rather than defining his own limits and abilities. He focused on his own power through his creative expression by becoming a pinball wizard, an activity that brought him love, joy, freedom, and self-respect. The symbolic lines in the song, "We're Not Gonna Take It," "Listening to you I hear the music, looking at you I feel the glory...," are a symbolic representation that we all must look within ourselves to find our own power through the positive expression of joy, freedom, self-worth, and love—qualities that are in each of us and enable us to live our lives with exhilarating passion if we so choose.

* * * * * * *

"I've envied him his freedom to step out in the full fury of his beliefs armed with a passion I'll never know or feel."

Prince of Tides by Pat Conroy

Perhaps one of the easiest and most practical ways to shift and change our mental focus into empowerment reframing is to simply become solution-focused in the way we evaluate and solve our problems. This is a very simple concept in which we focus our attention and behaviors on possible solutions to problems, rather than analyze the problem itself in great, historical detail. In psychotherapy, traditional psychoanalytical or psychodynamic therapy is based on long, relationship-developing periods of time in which the problems are extensively explored and analyzed to enhance awareness with the assumption that awareness will lead to change. But the reality is, as mentioned earlier, awareness does not lead to change but only leads to awareness. Change, although perhaps facilitated by the awareness, must be intended and exerted through a deliberate change in perceptions, thoughts, and behaviors after the awareness. In solution-focused or motivational, brief psychotherapy, the problem is acknowledged but not amplified, and attention focuses on solutions to that problem and motivating change toward that solution. This approach, pioneered by the late Milton Erickson, makes significant and often dramatic uses of positive refraining (empowerment reframing) and new, positive *neuro-associations*. It also serves as the basis for hypnotherapy, by using new positive images to make new positive *neuro-associations*. Perhaps the best way to illustrate this approach is through the use of an example. Let's take the case of Mark, the previously mentioned thirty-five year old man with TBI who was afraid to use the telephone. Traditional therapy would have approached the problem by a long, extensive analysis and clarification of the problem—when it began, what his old associations were, all the while cultivating a therapeutic relationship through the use of empathy and active listening. Ultimately, the "breakthrough" would occur when new associations replace the old ones and emphasis is on the need to change. But in solution-focused approaches, all that historical stuff can be cut through by getting right to the heart of the matter, that is, change (without sacrificing a positive relationship through empathic listening). In a solution-focused approach, I, the therapist, would simply ask Mark to imagine a miracle occurring and this problem he had with the telephone simply disappeared then and ask him to reflect on what he would notice about his life as being different. Mark, reflecting on this, would likely make statements such as, "I could handle my own problems and express things exactly as I want to," or, "I can get much more accomplished," or, "I would feel better about myself, taking care of my own problems rather than depending on other people." In effect, we are giving him a positive image, a new neuro-association to what the solution of that problem would look like: Then he would be asked how badly he wants to change this (how much pain does he get in his life by not changing), and then asked what he must do to acquire more confidence in changing toward a solution to that problem. The dialogue between the therapist and Mark might go something like this:

Therapist: Mark, let's say this miracle occurs and the problem simply disappears, what would you notice about your life being different?

Mark: I would have more self-confidence and be able to solve more of my own problems without having to wait for other people to be available.

Therapist: On a scale of one to ten, how big is this problem to you, one being very small and ten being very big?

Mark: About a seven.

Therapist: Now, again on a scale from one to ten, how badly do you want to change this, to find a solution for this problem? A one represents you don't want to change it at all and ten means you want to change it more than anything in the world.

Mark: Again, about a seven.

Therapist: Now here's the crucial question. How much confidence do you have that you can change this problem to become not a problem? A one represents very little confidence and ten means all the confidence in the world.

Mark: About a three, I don't have much confidence about changing it.

Therapist: Okay, then what do you think you need to do differently to change that three to about a four?

Mark: Hmmm.....Maybe I could arrange to have a phone conversation with someone with whom I feel safe and trust and seeing if its true that it is more difficult to understand me on the phone than it is in person.

Of course, this therapeutic exchange is oversimplified for purposes of illustration, but I think it gives the picture. And the beauty is that you don't have to go to therapy to become solution-focused. As a matter of fact, research has shown that most changes, or therapeutic changes, occur spontaneously without therapeutic intervention. We simply have to get in the habit of new empowerment reframing, and become solution, rather than problematic, focused. This perceptual and existential orientation to life and all of its inevitable problems in growth serves as a crucial difference between approaching a problem in a pessimistic, timid, apprehensive manner ("I'll never make enough money to travel the way I would really like to.") and an optimistic, positive, and empowered manner ("Let's see, I've decided I really want to go to Switzerland and ski. How am I going to do this? What's the first step I have to take?")

* * * * * * *

"In village life the blacksmith was second in importance only to the priest...by unwritten code he always hired a Catholic as his assistant and another as his apprentice...He ran Conor away 20 times but Conor returned at 21st."

Trinity by Leon Uris

To truly develop a sense of empowerment reframing, a new habit has to be acquired in which problems in living are repetitively and habitually approached with a positive mental focus, always attaching positive *neuro-associations* with positive change. In other words, to get into the mode that changing is more pleasurable than not changing. This type of internal "brainwashing" is crucial, possible, and is deemed only to lead to success and personal empowerment. You can think of your brain like a computerized tape player with thousands and thousands of scripts inside tiny audio microcassettes. A stimulus in the world occurs, whether it be another person's behavior or an event, and a button is pushed and a tape automatically gets played (script). Well, it is not only possible, but absolutely essential that negative tapes get changed to positive ones. You can also visualize your brain like a camera in which you focus on some things and not others. At any given moment in your conscious, daily life, you are focusing on certain things and excluding perhaps thousands of other things through the use of selective perception. We tend to evaluate, appraise, and behave based on the way this camera focuses on our external reality. For example, if we go to a party and our camera (brain) focuses primarily on another couple who seems to be avoiding us, we will inevitably leave that party evaluating it as a lousy, boring party. However, if we make the effort to continue refocusing to find something, no matter how small, that is positive in that party and focus entirely on that or entirely and only on other things that are positive, we will inevitably leave that party with a good feeling and evaluate it perhaps even as a smash. In our past lives, we may have been taught to develop negative audio tapes and negative camera focusing. We may have acquired negative, often unconscious, scripts and attitudes from our parents or other authority figures in our earlier years, or at least conflicting messages.

Consider the issue of money, for example. Some people attach positive and negative meanings to money and acquiring wealth and success. After hearing phrases from their parents such as, "Money is the root of all evil," or, "Money doesn't grow on trees," or, "Money just means you have to work very hard (pain)," and therefore attaching negative *neuro-associations* with money. This is often why many people sabotage their own success and ability to earn more money which would serve as a basis (an important distinction, a means rather than an end) for increased enjoyment, self-respect, freedom, and expression of love. But if we reprogram our brains to play only positive audio tapes and to focus that brain/camera only on positive associations and solutions, we inevitably will generate our ability to not only increase our success, but to enjoy it as well. However, despite any negative conditioning we may have acquired in our earlier years with respect to scripts and negative focusing, it is crucial to point out here that the past does not determine the present and the future, and we can choose to make positive, empowerment reframings of your consciousness by switching to positive tapes and positive focusing on positive solutions. But this change must come with a new, positive *neuro-association* which, again, emphasizes that change will be pleasurable and not to change will be painful.

One helpful way to position yourself for change, or as we discussed earlier, getting into the preparation stage for change, is to look for times, instances, or exceptions in your life when the problem was not a problem and focus on all of the variables which accounted for that state. A lot of these variables for these exceptions will include some changes in physiological states, as well as changes in mental focusing or, as we describe it, empowerment reframing. I'll share with you a personal experience as an example. In my earlier years, it was more difficult for me to initiate, cultivate and develop relationships, whether it involved social or friendship types of relationships or more intimate types. The root of the problem was that I feared rejection, or perhaps more appropriately, I feared not getting approval. I feared not only the deprivation of positive responses, but also feared acquiring negative responses, that is, being criticized, passively or aggressively, by others for things I did or the way I behaved. Thus, I was overly sensitive if I did not get some type of approval for the way I behaved, including adaptive measures that I had to use because of my disabilities such as a white cane, guide dog, mechanical listening devices, etc. This made it difficult for me to initiate and establish relationships, whether it meant going to a party or calling up a woman for a date. In other words, that was how the problem manifested itself to me. It was difficult for me to become more assertive and outgoing in my relationships for fear of their lack of approval which I would interpret as rejection. That was the problem. However, I also began thinking about how, at times, that problem was not a problem. I began thinking more about these exceptions and focusing on the positive, and thus, began thinking about how there were times, even if they were exceptions, that it was not difficult for me to go out to a party, or to call someone up on the phone for a date, or just to have a private lunch with someone. When I focused on what was different about those exceptions, I realized that I felt stronger, my physical state was stronger, that is, I felt alive, energetic, and confident. I also realized how my mental state, or tendencies towards an empowerment reframing, was also different in a positive sense. I reflected upon, not only thought about in my head but felt in my gut, how, during these exceptions, I did not worry that someone might decline my offer or they might be perceiving me in a negative manner. I knew, during these exceptions, that I was more centered, that is, my locus of control was more internal, rather than external. I reexperienced, actually relived, those exceptions until I felt all that power come throughout my whole being—my body and my mind. I even came to reframe in a different manner what it would mean if someone actually said no to my offer. I would still congratulate myself on completing my goal, that is, taking the risk and asking someone, or going somewhere that I was initially anxious about. This focusing on exceptions when current problems were less problematic in the past, even if only rare exceptions, can be valuable by allowing us to focus all of our positive physical and mental energy into a new positive direction.

Chapter Five

Empowerment Reframing—Developing New Neuro-Associations for Fear to Help Us with the Rocky Path of Life

It (Shibumi) is spiritual tranquillity without being passive, it is being without the (angst) of becoming, and in the personality of man it is, how does one say it, authority without domination...

"How does one achieve this Shibumi, sir?" (asked Nickolia)

"One does not achieve it, one discovers it."

From that moment Nickolia's primary goal in life was to become a man of Shibumi, a man of power.

Shibumi by Trevanian

This now leads us to a crucial discussion on the whole issue of *fear*. Although we have touched on the issue of fear in previous sections of this book, it is now necessary to give it a more thorough examination because fear is the major roadblock to change. As previously discussed, our goal in life, regardless of our activities, is to fulfill our physical and psychosocial needs. If we move in the direction of fulfilling our psychological needs, that is, to have fun, to feel important, to feel love, and to feel freedom, we arrive at pleasurable states, but if we do not move in positive directions, we move in the direction of painful states. That is, we could come to feel bored, lonely, trapped, or inadequate and rejected by others. Moving toward these painful states evokes fear—a necessary mechanism stimulated in our brains and we prepare for fight or flight from an activity or event that is associated with the fear of pain being evoked. Defense mechanisms are mental activities in which we flee in response to the fear that is associated with an event that, most likely, would trigger psychological pain. You may jump into an abusive or neglectful relationship to avoid the pain of loneliness, and we might use the defense mechanism of denial or rationalization about that relationship. We may deny that the relationship is abusive, or deny the fact that it really bothers us, or rationalize that it is really a beautiful relationship because we are so capable of being understanding to such an abusive partner. The major issue is that fear is the main motivator which propels us into negative states, so that they will not be painful. A blind individual may deal with the fear of isolation or the fear of being rejected by isolating himself, or choosing community activities which provide restricted social contact and environments. He may then deny that the isolation or restricted environment bothers him, or is painful, and rationalize that this behavior is necessary because these are the only options that are available.

Many times, the goal in therapy, regardless of the types of therapeutical approaches used, is to bring a client back to that point in time when he was confronted with the fearful situation, and made responses in negative, antigrowth directions, and then encourage the client to choose new behavioral responses in positive directions. The whole idea is that any time a fearful situation is encountered because of the pain of the negative psychosocial states (trapped, lonely, bored, or rejected), the person must move in a forward direction, a positive one, in order to develop the psychosocial maturation and greater internal control over his or her life. One of the best ways to facilitate and promote positive responses to fear in the anticipation of painful events is to make new meaning, new *neuro-associations*, with fear itself. Many times, with myself as well as with my clients in therapy, I have been taking a new, positive look at what fear is and what it means. When clients began expressing anxiety or nervousness about fearful situations such as asking someone out for a date, applying for new jobs—I would help them make a positive association with that fear, that is, to think of that fear as being good, think of it as being a desirable state, since it signifies readiness to move in a new, positive direction.

Fear is a state to be welcomed, for it signifies growth and challenges, new exciting ideas and possibilities. A famous old existential philosopher, Kierkegaard, once stated "the greater the number of possibilities, the greater the anxiety, so therefore the greater the anxiety, the greater the man." Giving fear new meaning means that you are actually welcoming it and are less likely to run from it or avoid it, which would only set up the likelihood of avoiding or burying the circumstance or event associated with the fear and making that event overwhelmingly fearful. I remember in my earlier days as a ski racer starting out, I would jump in the starting gate and, naturally, encounter the sensation of anxiety and fear and respond to that sensation by almost not wanting to be in the starting gate, wanting to avoid it. Then I made a new mental *neuro-association* with fear, giving it a positive, welcoming association and I later began actually looking forward to the starting gate and the fear associated with it.

Another way that is helpful to put fear into a positive, empowerment reframing is to reinforce the fear by reinforcing the activity that evoked the fear. For example, if someone in therapy came to a session reporting on taking a risk by calling someone else up for a date and was rejected and began to feel inadequate and rejected as a person, I would reframe that episode into a positive direction by having the client focus not on the outcome of the offer for the date, which was a declining of the date, but focusing positively on encountering the fear, picking up the phone, making the call, and requesting a date. All those activities are within one's control, and can be positively reinforced, and therefore, set up within the parameters of the goal. That is, the goal becomes picking up the phone and asking someone for a date, not actually acquiring a date or someone else responding affirmatively to the request for the date. In effect, we are shifting the goal to what is in our internal locus of control rather than our external locus of control.

For a subliminal effect, I will repeat that the goal is picking up the phone and making the call, not the actual acquisition of a date because of the person's affirmative response. Again, this internal locus of control sets the basis for true empowerment, thus empowerment reframing means making positive neuro-associations with the fear that we can do what we wish to do, despite our fear. Fear has a positive association because it signals that we are about to make an empowerment move.

Many of us are familiar with the famous and beautiful quote, "God grant me the serenity to accept the things that I cannot change, the courage to change the things that I can, and the wisdom to know the difference." In fact, this is a beautiful, poetic reference to the fight-flight mechanism evoked by fear. At the moment you become fearful or frightened by someone or something, you must make a decision whether to fight (confront, change) or flight (flee, avoid, withdraw, etc.). Both responses, in fact, are action or change responses. The key issue here is that appraisal of what it is we are encountering. More important, the wiser or more wisdom we have, or the more psychosocial maturation we have, the greater our ability to appraise the reality of the situation in our world objectively. This relates very much to our perceptions and our *neuro-associations* and accounts for why one blind individual can approach the tasks of learning Braille or socially integrating with the community, whereas another blind individual avoids learning Braille and remains socially isolated. It has to do with level of psychosocial maturation, or interdependence and an internal locus of control rather than dependence and an external locus of control in meeting psychosocial (as well as physical) needs.

* * * * * * *

"Some men can overcome tragedy, even attain greatness because of it. Most men can't and the Bogside is full of those."

Trinity by Leon Uris

Here it is important to differentiate between fear and panic. Simply speaking, fear is an emotional state in which one feels uncomfortable and anxious, but the emotion is manageable, whereas panic is a full-blown fear that is out of control and unmanageable. What differentiates between fear and panic is the way in which we respond at the moment we encounter the fear. Consider the example of a visualized situation. Imagine yourself swimming across a river that is about one mile wide and about halfway across you begin to develop cramps in your legs. The cramps in your legs signal a threatening situation and you respond with the feeling of fear that prepares you for action. The healthy response to this signal of fear is realizing that, in fact, you do have cramps in your legs and must take immediate action to confront them. Thus, you might take slow deep breaths, stop swimming momentarily, even take gulps of air to submerge yourself under water so you can massage your cramped legs, and other remedial approaches. The fear has signaled that you must do something constructively to solve the problem. Now, part of your ability to confront this fear constructively had depended on your sense of confidence about how to deal with the problem, you may even have had prior information on how to handle cramps while swimming. But even this might not have been necessary, as sometimes confronting a fear constructively means just having an overall sense of an ability to be able to confront fearful situations positively.

Now, consider a different response to the same situation.

Imagine yourself swimming and you again confront the cramps in your legs. This time, because of an unconscious or conscious sense that there is nothing you can do about it independently or even just a vague sense that you don't have much ability to handle anything on your own (independently, interdependently), you ignore the fear either by denying (repressing into your unconscious) or rationalizing that there is nothing wrong because this happens all the time and therefore you continue swimming. Of course, if you continue swimming the cramp will only worsen despite the psychological defenses, and eventually the pain of the cramp will be so great that you can no longer ignore it either in denial or by rationalization. When this happens and the defenses no longer work and there is still a sense that there is nothing you can do about it, that is, you are helpless in the situation that is out of control, then panic (rather than manageable fear) will set in. Of course, when panic sets in, the stress is so out of control and unmanageable that inevitable regression to earlier forms of development (even at infancy levels) occurs, and the behavior follows suit accordingly. Thus, you would recoil, scream or thrash about senselessly, hoping for someone or something to save you, that is, to take care of you.

Now, another important issue about fear is that we not only respond to it when we actually encounter it, but we also respond to anticipated fear, that is, we respond to events or situations that we anticipate or expect to be painful or threatening to our physical or psychological well-being. Simply speaking, in the case of swimming, what this means is that you anticipate the activity of swimming to be stressful, but manageable, and you swim anyway or to be so stressful (physically and/or psychologically) and beyond your control (an anticipated panic situation) that you avoid the activity. When this happens, we are probably unaware of the lack of pleasure from denying or depriving ourselves of the activity of swimming by the defense mechanism of denial or rationalization, but we are still restricting opportunities for fulfilling the important psychosocial need of fun and enjoyment. That is, we are depriving ourselves of the expanded options and flexibility in having control over meeting one of our important psychosocial needs. Now, getting back to the famous quotation of, "...grant me the serenity to accept the things I cannot change, the courage to change the things that I can...," there perhaps are some people who actually are psychosocially mature who are simply unable to swim because of real limits, perhaps because of quadriplegia, no arms, etc. This is simply a situation of accepting something they cannot change, but it still does not mean that there are not many other options for their psychosocial need for fun as well as many other options for the other psychosocial needs. However, there also may be other disabled individuals, such as someone who is blind, paraplegic, etc., who believe they are unable to swim; that is, they are looking through the eyes and experiencing things as an individual with immature psychosocial maturation and thus fleeing from the situation rather than fighting (confronting) the situation to master the task of swimming, and a potentially enjoyable means of fulfilling the psychosocial need for fun. I emphasize the word potential, because you really don't know whether it's enjoyable until the activity has been tried out. In some cases, there may be some substitute water activities for that person who objectively and maturely (wisely) decides that he cannot swim, which may constructively be substituted to meet the psychosocial need for fun. Such activities could include boating, fishing or even snorkeling.

* * * * * * *

"...The person who is normal in terms of being well-adapted is often less healthy than the neurotic person in terms of human values. Often he is well-adapted only at the expense of giving up his self in order to become more

91

or less the person he believes he is expected to be. All genuine individuality and spontaneity may have been lost. One the other hand the neurotic person can be characterized as someone who is not willing to surrender completely in the battle for 'self'...and instead of expressing himself productively he sought salvation through neurotic symptoms and by withdrawing in to a fantasy life. Nevertheless from the standpoint of human values he is less crippled than the kind of 'normal' person who has lost his individuality altogether. The relevance is to 'group thing' in America."

Escape from Freedom by Erich Fromm

One of the major goals in empowerment development is learning new, positive ways to confront fear when it is encountered. The old saying is so true, "the greatest fear is fear itself." That is, the moment fear is confronted, accept it and challenge it with manageable perceptual and behavioral responses, rather than avoiding a nonchallenge by either denying its existence or perceiving that it is too great to overcome. Many people have approached me after I have done something they consider quite remarkable such as skiing a long, steep downhill course or the KT-22 at Squaw Valley (the 14th steepest slope in the world) and say to me that I must not be afraid of anything. That is very untrue. I am fearful and apprehensive when I approach these situations, but somehow find a way to make a positive neuro-association with the fear to unleash both my enthusiasm and positive emotions as well as my careful, intellectual judgment as to how I will confront and accomplish the challenge. Remember, the excitement and enthusiasm of the challenge, like the wind in the sails of the ship, is ineffective and possibly dangerous unless the intellect helps to manage the challenge, like the rudder of the ship. If I skied the dangerous downhill or KT-22 without any prior skill or physical conditioning and training, that would be most likely because of encountering the fear senselessly, perhaps denying it through the defense mechanism of overcompensation. The issue is:

fear must be given new positive associations, breaking old conditioning habits of avoiding situations when encountering fear, creating new patterns of confronting the situation when encountering the fear by giving it a positive neuro-association. If we don't do this, we are likely to deny the fear and the source of it and ultimately let that fear bottle up in our subconscious until we can no longer avoid it and thus create a panic situation. Getting in the habit of approaching fear this constructive way is mental conditioning toward the process of psychosocial maturation, developing the ability to meet psychosocial needs interdependently and becoming stronger, the same way we become stronger physically by physical conditioning.

A good method in making this positive *neuro-association* with fear is to understand that growing needs encountering new situations and thus, is in itself fearful. Anyone who has read Gail Sheehy's classic book *Passages* understands this. To grow throughout the life cycle means to change and to acquire new things at the expense of "giving up" old things and ideas (as I have discussed in the introduction of this book). Take a simple example. Consider a professional athlete who no longer can meet his psychosocial needs for fun and self-worth because he is becoming too old to play professional football and thus must "give up" the activity. If he has an adequate degree of psychosocial maturation or interdependence to meet his psychosocial needs he would adequately, after some manageable stress, find a new alternative to meeting these needs by other activities. On the contrary, if he did not have adequate development, he would respond to this fearful situation initially by denying that his aging body is performing less skillfully, but then would most likely encounter panic or near panic when sidelined by his coach and replaced by a younger player. This is the difference between the guy who responds to the fearful situation by making such statements as, "Well, I have to give up skiing. There's nothing I can do," and sits home, broods, becomes socially isolated and depressed; as opposed to the guy who makes statements like, "Uhm, I can no longer ski but what other activities are there that I can do for fun and feel good about myself? I think I'll try them out even if they will make me feel nervous and like a beginner," and approaches these activities with apprehension, but enthusiasm and positive attitudes.

* * * * * * *

"...I stayed up the night and knew I had passed an important week in my life. I had been married for almost six years, had established my career as a teacher and coach, and was living out my life as a mediocre man."

Prince of Tides by Pat Conroy

What we are about to discuss here is an important issue and related to what we have been talking about with respect to fear. For many people, they only have a few, perhaps only one way or maybe even no ways, to meet one of their psychosocial needs, and they make positive neuro-associations with this condition. Again, let's use another example to illustrate this important fact. Suppose a disabled individual only one relationship, such as a family member, to meet her psychosocial need for love and belonging and thus, tends to be socially isolated. What makes defense mechanisms work is that they give positive neuro-associations with these negative states. That is, a positive neuro-association is given to the condition of being isolated by either denying the reality and the pain of isolation or rationalizing the isolation by giving it a positive association such as saying, "It's good to only have one person that you are close to because that means you are really close to someone, sort of like the principle of having a few or only one close friend rather than a lot of acquaintances."

A crucial and important step in empowerment development, or empowerment reframing, is to break the pattern of giving positive *neuro-associations* to negative situations with respect to the fulfillment of psychosocial needs. Simply speaking, we must face the reality and confront the truth that it is not positive to be bored or have one or no friends, to feel inadequate or to feel trapped. Defense mechanisms can give positive associations with negative states and thus, often create mixed and confusing messages. For example, we may say things to ourselves like, "It is okay to be successful, but we don't want to be too successful because that is being selfish," or, "It is okay to have fun, but not too much fun because that is selfish," or, "It is okay to love someone, but not too much because I will deprive myself." There are, of course millions of situations, and the point is that we begin to sabotage or short circuit our growth by beginning to assign negative neuro-associations with growth or positive neuro-associations with the lack of growth. Again, empowerment is the process of breaking these habits of assigning positive neuro-associations to lack of growth and negative neuro-associations toward the process of growth. It is essentially this dynamic in its extreme case that makes some people associate pleasure with such growth stifling conditions as physical abuse and pain with growth enhancing situations.

* * * * * * *

"How do you suppose he does it? I don't know...that deaf, dumb and blind kid sure plays a mean pinball."
Pinball Wizard by Elton John

Now to get to the summation of all this. What is necessary to become empowered to reach our fullest potential and become truly alive is that we must respond to the inevitable signal of fear by making pleasurable associations with growth and painful associations with delay of growth or absence of growth. This may sound contradictory because we have earlier said that to grow is fearful and painful, but what I mean is that, although there is some pain in the process of growth, overall it will bring on more pleasure than pain. Likewise, although there is some pleasure in the absence of growth, overall there would be more pain not to grow than pleasure. What we

95

are simply doing is giving new associations to fear and pain in the process of growth. They are positive and pleasurable associations and we are giving new meaning to pleasure in the lack of growth, that is, that the pleasure in not growing is really painful, not pleasurable. This brings us to the important concept of delay of immediate gratification.

As mentioned earlier, all this concept means is that, if we delay or defer immediate pleasure, we will gain greater pleasure in the long run or, if we defer or delay immediate pain, we will gain greater pain in the long run. Consider dieting and weight control to illustrate this principle. If we defer the immediate pleasure of eating the ice cream, we will gain the greater pleasure in the long run of feeling in better shape and more alive, and having a better self-image. Thus we are giving a new neuro-association to that "pleasurable" state of eating the ice cream and now assigning it a negative neuro-association, a painful condition. On the other hand, if we jump on the exercise bicycle and begin to experience the pain of working out, we give that pain a new positive *neuro-association*. It is a pleasurable sense, that is, we relish the pain, feel good about it because we know it leads to a greater internal locus of control and greater psychosocial maturation that is, overall, a greater pleasurable state. When we get in the habit of making these new *neuro-associations*, we are conditioning ourselves in the habit of positioning for and actually making new positive changes. It prepares us for the fight-flight mechanism (action mechanism) more realistically and constructively and gives us a greater sense of control (internal locus of control), psychosocial maturation and self-esteem. I believe it is important to differentiate between self-esteem and self-confidence. Self-confidence is actually one of our psychosocial needs, having confidence that we can accomplish things and make a contribution to the world and have self-worth, whereas self-esteem is valuing ourselves highly because of our overall ability to meet all of our psychosocial needs interdependently and having an overall sense of maturity and wisdom.

Chapter Six

Developing Our Healthy Egos— Meeting Our Needs By Focusing On Solutions Rather Than Problems

Pico della Mirandola, "Oratio de Hominis Dignitate: 'Neither heavenly or earthly, neither mortal nor immortal have we created thee, so that thou mightest be free according to thy own will and honor, to be thy own creator and builder. To thee alone we gave growth and development depending on thy own free will. Thou bearest in thee the germs of a universal life.'"

Escape from Freedom by Erich Fromm

Now, what about the goal of successfully getting through the grieving process associated with our disabilities, and how does that fit in with all these other goals we have identified connected to our psychosocial needs? In other words, have you successfully resolved the goal of grieving, that is, getting through the pain of the disabling condition to the other end and accepting the disability, or have you avoided or withdrawn from this pain and set up positive neuro-associations with the defenses (such as denial, rationalization or overcompensation) associated with activities related to the avoidance? One possible way you can answer this is by looking at the types of goals you have formulated for yourself, as well as a close personal examination.

If you have developed goals for yourself that are relatively minimal and do not provide you with a good deal of enthusiasm once you have projected yourself into the future and considered having attained them, chances are you probably have not resolved the grieving process because you are probably operating in the belief system that you are not a whole and/or worthy person. In other words, you are probably not a person with a relatively high degree of psychosocial maturation, one who is able to meet their needs interdependently and has an internal locus of control. On the other hand, if you have selected goals that seem to be challenging and major to you and provide you with a sense of enthusiasm at the thought of attaining them, chances are you are looking at yourself with a belief system predicated with high self-esteem, that is as an individual with a higher degree of psychosocial maturation and an internal locus of control. But I do believe that the goal of getting through the grieving process is best accomplished more indirectly, that is, you accomplish that goal by a direct approach to fulfilling your physical and psychosocial needs interdependently, and the grieving process will resolve itself. This is because if we focus too much on the disabling condition and whether we got through the pain of the loss, we will become more problem focused or problem saturated mainly because there is absolutely nothing that can be done to change the disabling condition itself. But as we seek to attain other goals in the psychosocial domain, we can approach these goals with a new empowerment reframing, that is, a positive physical and mental focus which gives new meaning to the disability. By giving the disability such as loss of sight new meaning, we are not denying the disability or how we feel about it through rationalizations, overcompensation and the like, we are simply giving new positive meaning to a diffi-cult situation.

For example, we could say that the disability is presenting us with clear challenges for physical and mental strengthening, or as an opportunity to help others go through difficult situations, or whatever, without the sacrifice of the idea that we are still worthy, dignified and whole people. Part of the reason I choose not to focus directly on the goal of getting through the grieving process is be-cause it is almost like constantly taking your temperature to see if you are ill (or taking an emotional temperature to see if you are emotionally ill) which only keeps you focused on the idea of the problem. It is similar to the idea of dieting (deprivation of food) which only reminds people of food, something they are trying to avoid, and perpetrates their consciousness of the problem. When I have had overweight clients in therapy, I have them focus on goals they wish to accomplish rather than on dieting itself. Focusing on dieting itself focuses on deprivation of food which is essentially fo-cusing on the problem rather than on the solutions and thus "trig-gers" problematic behavior. Similarly, focusing on the grieving process itself focuses consciousness on the disability which, again, is focusing on the problem rather than the solution, "triggering" problematic behavior. This occurs, in part, because just being fully able-bodied does not necessarily guarantee the unleashing toward psychosocial growth and maturation of attitudes and the motiva-tion to make changes. The ability to see or walk, as stated earlier, are not *ends* in themselves as being the source of capacities to change our physical and mental states, rather they are *means*. Similarly, not being overweight or not suffering from compulsive eating does not assure capabilities for changing physical and/or mental states, and thus not being overweight is not an *end* in itself with respect to posi-tive emotions and motivation, but rather is a *means*.

We can also understand this dynamic of focusing on the wrong problem and asking the wrong questions if we look at it in another way. It took me years of study and practice to understand fully the concepts of psychological theory and dynamics, but I will try to translate some basic concepts to you as simply as possible. I have been talking about maturity as being the capability to handle one's own physical and psychosocial needs interdependently, that is, while we are able to care for and manage our own physical and psychosocial states, the more mature we are and the greater our internal locus of control, the greater our empowerment. In psychological jargon we call this psychosocial maturation, which is a process of developing ego strength. In classical psychoanalytical theory, there is a child with all of his creative and destructive impulses which are defined as the id. Then there are the parents and other authority figures who impose guidance and limitations which are called the super ego. Hopefully, in between is the ego, or the independent or reality-testing aspect of the growing child, which will develop into full maturity. It is the strengthening ego that determines the growing child's and growing individual's capabilities to be able to manage their lives independently by adequate reality-testing and decision making (problem solving). The theory of transactional analysis uses the concept similarly but with different language, referring to the previously three mentioned dynamics—id, ego, super ego—as simply the *child, adult, and parent.*

The goal of growth and maturation is to develop healthy egos or adult components within us. We also do not want to completely dispose of the child and parent aspects of our lives since there are positive, healthy elements of these components. It is through the child that we become fun loving, spontaneous and creative (as well as impulsive and destructive), and it is through the parent that we can assimilate through positive role modeling advice, information and rules about our society and world through our parents and authority figures.

But sometimes we hear messages coming through our parent or super ego part of the personality which only trigger impulsive and destructive responses from the child without the intervention of the adult (or ego). For example, the process of dieting usually triggers a message from the parent of the personality that one must not or should not eat. This, in turn, triggers either a compliance or rebellious message from the child without allowing for the intervention of the adult. This destructive mechanism will most likely inhibit the developing adult to evaluate and make appraisals about the adult's (ego) major responsibility—finding more adequate and suitable ways to fulfill physical and psychosocial needs since dieting has nothing to do with it simply because dieting is a means rather than an end for fulfilling psychosocial needs. In other words, the adult ego asks and evaluates such questions as, "How will dieting and losing weight change the quality of my life (my ability to meet my physical and psychosocial needs)?" or "What will I be able to do (think, feel and/or behave) differently as a result of losing weight and not overeating?" or, "Why can't I just go ahead and do the things I would like to do or be the way I would like to be whether I lose weight or not?" Questions and evaluations of this nature would likely lead to more constructive problem-solving and solution-focused behavior rather than focusing on the dieting itself. Focusing on dieting, food deprivation, counting calories, etc., only distracts from the real purpose of the ego, or the developing level of psychosocial maturation, and is more likely to trigger negative responses from the id (child), such as guilt, shame, overcompliance, and rebellion without allowing for adequate intervention and development of the ego (adult). I remember once I had the most progress with a woman who came to therapy for overeating by having her focus on the equestrian lessons she planned to take if the weight loss occurred rather than on the dieting itself.

Similarly, focusing directly and too much on whether a disability has been successfully grieved is focusing too much on the disability and the inability or ability to cope with it which is focusing on the problem. This focus of attention is likely to elicit messages from the parent (super ego), that one must grieve successfully or one should grieve successfully, thereby, distracting one from the real issues that successful grieving is only a *means* toward the goal of enabling one to meet his own psychosocial needs interdependently, not an end in itself. This focusing attention on the grieving distracts and inhibits the process of the developing adult (ego). Back to the dieting analogy, when people begin focusing on how to meet their psychosocial needs directly, which is finding ways to have fun and feel self-worth, the dieting and impulsive overeating (symptoms) usually recede and eventually terminate. Similarly, when the business of maturing and acquiring an internal locus of control in meeting one's own physical and psychosocial needs continues and carries on, problems in grieving usually recede and terminate. This is not to imply that it is not helpful to clarify and give new meaning to the grieving process, but doing this in more of an acknowledging sense rather than in an amplifying, problem saturated sense is the key to successful grief resolution. You can monitor successful grief resolution from time to time simply by seeing how adequately you are getting on with the business of taking care of yourself and your needs in a constructive, interdependent and solution-focused manner.

Now, let's take one goal you have selected for yourself. Take one that seems highly important, something you really want to accomplish within the next six months or a year. Under that goal I would like you to list all the advantages there are for you by not completing that goal. Think of the benefits associated with not completing that goal, such as not having to endure the stress and the discomfort, or to delay it. Now think of all the disadvantages you acquire or the liabilities you acquire from not completing that goal. Think of the pleasure you will lose out on by not completing the goal. Before you were thinking of the pain you were avoiding by not striving to accomplish a goal. Now, think of all the pain you will acquire, the disadvantages, by striving towards that goal. List all the discomforts and the things you anticipate will hurt you by the successful completion of the goal. Then think of all the benefits and advantages you will acquire by the successful completion of the goal, or the pleasure. We are simply going back to our pleasure-pain principle and the neuro-associations we are making with it.

I will give you an example. My own goal is writing this book which establishes a goal. The goal was to write an empowerment book. The advantages in not meeting this goal or writing the book is that I could delay or defer making a commitment, taking the time to sit down and to think about ideas and actually start writing or be distracted from other things I like doing like reading novels, eating or overeating. The disadvantage in not taking action and taking steps toward the successful completion of that goal is that I acquired the unsettling feeling of procrastination, a sense like meaningful time was passing me by, a sense of emptiness or blank space or unmeaningful activities and a sense of a lack of challenge. The advantages for taking action and starting toward a successful completion of writing the book was that I acquired a pleasurable sense of challenge, a sense of satisfaction of working to develop constructive thoughts and new ideas about myself and others, increasing my sense of self-worth like I am contributing something, at times, a sense of · enjoyment through learning, a feeling of creative expression, and a feeling of caring and the ability to help others. The disadvantages of carrying through toward this goal were the structuring of time, the mental activity required, the work, the constructive criticism, etc.

The purpose for listing and tallying these advantages and disadvantages for not accomplishing the goal and accomplishing the goal is that it helps us to get positioned and ready for action. It brings to the consciousness and the forefront of our awareness some old, unconscious habits of procrastinating and delaying and denying our own growth. It makes more vivid and visible our negative empowerment habits, our lack of mental and physical refocusing, or our lack of empowerment reframing. What is important now is to go over all of the advantages or pleasures you have listed for not accomplishing the goal. Here, a positive *neuro-association* has been given to a negative condition. You have assigned pleasurable meaning to lack of growth. Similarly, negative or painful meaning has been assigned to growth. To accomplish growth you want to amplify and focus with your consciousness to assist you with the solution of problems. The best way perhaps to do this is to focus always on the power and the pleasure you acquire in the accomplishment of your goals that lead to a greater sense of and control over meeting your psychosocial needs. To facilitate this, it is helpful to reassign a new positive meaning to the pain and fear that is associated with the acquisition of the goal. In the component where you have assigned painful meaning to the accomplishment of the goal, you want to get into empowerment reframing by making a new pattern, disrupting the old pattern and giving positive associations to the pain and fear that are necessary for the accomplishment of the goal. Rather than thinking, "Oh boy, writing this book is going to take time, cost me a lot of effort and energy with hard work," and let your physical state get into a tense anxious position, you want to make a new positive association, a positive mental focus and shift into a positive physical state about the excitement and enthusiasm that writing such a book will bring. Believe me, I do this all the time. This is not a matter of denying the reality of the pain or the existence of the pain through a defense mechanism such as denial, rationalization and other compensation, but rather, you are acknowledging the pain and giving it new meaning and making new positive neuro-associations. Denying the existence and the reality that is associated with the pain would, most likely, only lead to overexertion and burnout.

What we are doing here is enhancing motivation through the most positive preparation for change. Basically, this is done by focusing and literally visualizing with a clear image of what the expected outcome is with respect to the goal. This is done through a mental amplification of what it is we will accomplish through the attainment of the goal combined with a physical change of state in a positive direction along with a renewed mental refocusing of the previous negative associations into a positive *neuro-association*. The combination of these three elements literally makes for the parameters of the empowerment reframing toward taking action immediately. I do this all the time and it works, time and time again, for me. It is this basis, this capacity for mental and physical refocusing in positive directions that has literally accounted for all of my successes. What is occurring is "cutting through" all of the difficulties, the problem formulations and the problem assessments which confuse and negate the clear image of the successful outcome. Using an analogy, it is a clear amplification of the visual image of what the experience would be like skiing on a mountain in the beautiful crisp air, being with friends you care about, while giving little acknowledgment (without denying) to the stresses that are necessary to accomplish that task (such as the long drive, waking up early in the morning, the cost, etc.). In a sense, it is similar to when I practiced hypnotherapy and asked the clients to visualize a clear mental image, auditorily and/or visually, of what would occur when the goal is accomplished.

* * * * * * *

"Their American colleagues envisioned a world where states would act as cooperative partners, not as distrustful rivals. American leaders rejected the European ideas that the morality of states should be judged by different ideas than the morality of individuals. According to Jefferson, there existed but one system of ethics for men and for nations, generous, promoting in the long run even the interests of both."

Diplomacy by Henry Kissinger

The next step is taking action, immediate concrete action towards the achievement of that goal.

Now, the need domain on which I would like you to focus first is the one for love and belonging. The reason for that is because it is this area that not only fulfills an important psychosocial need, but also simultaneously provides for the development of healthy support systems, an area that is so crucial for the disabled toward the goal of becoming independent (interdependent), mastering the ability to meet psychosocial needs interdependently and, hence, successfully resolving the grieving process. It is so crucial for people with disabilities to develop an adequate, flexible network of relationships, formal and informal and to live successfully in the community. It is not only a matter of the most improved quality of life, it is also simply a matter of physical and psychosocial survival to develop relationships that are trusting and reciprocal with respect to give and take. It is also in this area that "role modeling" is going to be so crucial, and you will find by making positive use of this concept you will not only acquire significant role models for yourself but eventually will become role models for others. This point will be elaborated later. Now, looking under your columns for love and belonging, can you find an activity or a relationship circumstance which you have not only prioritized in that category, but have also described as a secondary role in another need column? For example, you may have indicated that you want to develop friendship relationships or improve an existing friendship relationship or two, and also notice, for fun, you wish to take up the activity of skiing. Or, it could be conversely, that you have prioritized the activity of skiing with a secondary benefit of cultivating a new friendship relationship. By the way, I don't want you to get too technical and too caught up in the technicalities of prioritizing and listing these activities and circumstances to meet psychosocial needs. This exercise is simply intended to assist you in focusing your thinking and behavior. Or you may have listed as wanting to improve your relationship with a family member or a roommate and it could have secondary gains for your sense of self-worth or your sense of enjoyment. In any event, the first thing I would like you to do is to take that one relationship you would like to either develop or improve and list all the advantages that you will gain putting in the effort to improve that relationship and then list all the disadvantages you will have by not putting in that effort. Now, I emphasize the phrase "putting in the effort" because it is important to recognize that no one has control over a relationship, you only have control over what you put into it. You can put in 100 percent and do all the right things to a perfect degree, and there is still no guarantee that the relationship outcome will be positive or satisfactory. To shift a goal to behavior changes on your part rather than relationship outcome, you will shift to an "internal locus of control" and feel more empowerment.

Consider the fact that one individual does all the healthy and "right" things in either developing or improving a new relationship; that is he is friendly, cordial, sensitive, interested, truthful, and the whole works, and yet the outcome of the relationship is still negative. It is up to that individual with whom we are putting the effort into the relationship to reciprocate in order to make possible simply because the other individual must do his or her share. Now the important fact about this is that it is equally important that the "giving" individual does not misinterpret the negative relationship . outcome to mean that he is inadequate, rejected, a failure, etc., but rather, the other individual has some problems of his or her own that have to be successfully resolved before a successful relationship outcome is possible. This fact is also crucial for the disabled.

Now, I want you to think hard about the very first step that you must take to initiate the development or improvement of this relationship. A good way to do this, after you have become positioned by considering the advantages and disadvantages, is to become solution-focused. I am going to give you a general rule of the universe with respect to empowerment. With any problem you have in life, no matter how big or small, twenty percent of your time should be spent thinking about the problem and the nature of it and eighty percent of your time should be thinking about the solution to that problem. Thus, if you have a problematic relationship with another or a generalized problem that you don't have enough relationships, just spend significantly smaller portions of the time thinking about the problem, its analysis, problem saturated formulations, and much more substantial time should be given to focusing on solutions or possible solutions to that problem. A major reason for this has to do with the previous discussion we had on the parent, adult, and child concepts (id, ego, and superego). In getting to the framework of thinking only about the problem and its analysis, we consciously or unconsciously get into a mental mode that we "have to" do something about it, that we must do something about it similar to the way the parent part of our personality communicates to our child part. This, of course, triggers negative *neuro-associative* responses and thus negative behavior responses such as over compliance, rebellion (actively or in the form of procrastination). When we focus on solutions, we develop a positive neuro-association and become much more aware of possibilities and choices, thus giving more positive neuro-associations with the situation leading to positive behaviors. In that sense, becoming solution-focused allows much greater opportunity for the development of the *adult* personality component, or the ego.

A good way to initiate this solution-focused approach, that is getting on track with a positive *neuro-association* in the direction of solutions, is to simply ask yourself what you expect to happen when the problem ceases. You can have some fun with this by pretending a miracle situation has occurred and the problem disappeared. Consider this situation. You go to bed tonight and this miracle occurs and the problem of not having a trustworthy, supportive relationship or having a problematic relationship disappears when you wake up in the morning. What would you notice? What would be different in your life? How would you feel? What do you think others would notice about you? What do you think others, including the person with whom you wish to have a relationship, would notice about you? How would you feel in other areas of your life such as your community, school, or work life? When you have considered all these aspects of how your life would be different and what you would notice about that if this miracle occurs, then you might want to consider to yourself how big is this problem to you or how stressful is it and actually rank it on a scale from one to ten, a one being not stressful at all and a ten being extremely stressful. Similarly, you may want to ask yourself how motivated you are to change this problem into not being a problem, with one being no motivation at all and ten meaning extremely motivated. Finally, you will want to ask yourself how much confidence you have in your ability to change this problem into a solution with a one representing very little confidence and ten representing all the confidence in the world. To consider this confidence aspect, you may also want to consider times in your life when there's an exception to this problem. Have there been times when you were able to get along with the family member or friend that you usually have a problem with or times that you were able to initiate the development of a new relationship? What did you do differently? How did you make that happen? What were your beliefs, your attitudes, your feelings, and your behavior that put you in control of initiating a positive relationship? You can think about this either before or after your disability. What matters is thinking about what you did, perceptually, mentally, and behaviorally, to affect this change. After considering all of this, then get back to the confidence issue and evaluate yourself. Now if you have evaluated yourself at a three indicating not too much confidence, think about what you have to do differently to change this into a four. What will you have to do differently, and how can you bring this into your control, into your empowerment? Then think about all the things that we have been discussing, changing your physical and your mental state into a new empowerment reframing and changing your old negative habits and changing your unproductive, negative beliefs such as "I'm not capable of having friends, who wants to be friends with someone who is disabled?" Once you have decided what you must do to raise that confidence level just a bit higher (just one step higher), take action NOW. DO IT. Don't think about it, just do it despite any residue of a conflict, and if there is a residue of a conflict start giving it a positive *neuro-association* saying, "THIS STRESS, THIS FEAR IS GOOD. It signifies that I am about to move into a positive direction." You are taking an empowerment step. So, suppose you have decided you want to call up a friend to do something together or come to visit you at your home, or you visit him at his home, do that now. If it is not possible to do it now, write down NOW and assign yourself the time exactly you will make that call and do it at that time. No hesitation, just do it. Start a positive new habit by the procrastination of procrastination. Develop the new empowerment habits of taking action, small steps at a time, but powerful actions nevertheless. This is a habit you want to get into. These are the steps of the new empowerment reframing of your life, getting on track to making your life work for you, being in control of your life and having "internal locus of control" so that you can meet your physical and psychosocial needs interdependently. These are basically the steps you will take in all of your goals and your solution-focused attempts to solving problems. Get in the habit. Continuously ask yourself do I really want to live or do I want to die (mentally or physically). Get back into your enthusiastic mode, fantasizing, if you wish, thinking about what you want out of life, pretending you're a child at Christmas again and all of the joy and positive emotion you feel about the things that you want. These kinds of fantasies, although not always able to be actualized, will give us important clues to what turns us on. You may not be able to become a professional athlete, but you could get into an associated activity with respect to your enjoyment or even a career if you should so desire. Risk taking for these endeavors are now not going to be considered negatively stressful, but positive.

In the appendices section to follow, I will be outlining and listing a variety of resources, basically formal and informal entities (organizations, agencies, self-help groups, foundations, etc.) which are typically used by people with disabilities as well as some entities that are not typically used by people with disabilities that could be beneficial to the disabled, and I want you to approach, explore, and use these resources in an attitude of empowerment. In other words, I want you to approach and explore and use these resources with a positive physical and mental state, a state of being in conditioning in which you become solution- rather than problem-focused where you will acquire that internal locus of control and truly feel empowered. For far too long, it appears obvious to me that there is an underlying assumption with respect to resources that help the disabled and that assumption is that it is the responsibility of these resources to take care of the disabled. That is very untrue, and it is only that type of thinking that leads to irresponsibility, immaturity, and a sense of powerlessness with an external sense of control. Even with entities set up to provide basic protection, financial or otherwise, for the disabled, such as social security, which are governed by laws, it is the responsibility of the disabled individual and their advocates (family members, other helpers) to insure that these responsibilities are carried through. In the wake of the independent living movement and the Americans With Disabilities Act (ADA), there has been a growing use of the term "consumer" to describe the disabled individual eligible for and benefiting from services. This word is basically selected, accurately so, to put the disabled individual's role in the proper perspective in that it is the consumer's responsibility to determine and to choose for which services and goods he is eligible for and could possibly benefit. It is the disabled individual's, the consumer's, responsibility to explore, solicit, or obtain services or goods that are helpful to meeting his physical and psychosocial needs and to live independently in the community, or at least, make independent decisions about how he will live, community or otherwise. The process of acquiring services and goods to help disabled individuals is just that—a process. The process, for the highest degree of personal satisfaction, must be developed with the basic assumption that it is the consumer's responsibility not only to explore, select and utilize resources, but to use them in a manner that truly facilitates his own physical and psychosocial well-being as well as his own growth. This attitude is somewhat similar to the changing trends in the doctor-patient relationship these days. You, most likely, know that years ago the doctor/patient relationship was characterized by the passive, often intimidated, patient submitting before the all-knowing, powerful doctor with the patient answering and not asking questions and, thus, not actively participating in the health care process. Today, patients have been changing their roles and becoming more assertive, aggressive, and participatory in their own treatment, challenging and questioning doctor's judgments on which they are either confused or in disagreement. This is not to imply that the doctor-patient relationship is antagonistic and one of conflict, but rather, a relationship characterized more by equality in which each has his responsibilities in order to participate in the health care process. In earlier years, rehabilitation used to be characterized with this "medical model" approach. It is the disabled individual conforming to and complying with most of or all of the authoritative rehabilitation counselors or other expert roles, but that is changing radically these days, not only for the purpose of benefiting the disabled individual's rehabilitation, but to establish and reinforce his dignity as well. While serving on a Statewide Independent Living Council (which I still do), we uncovered an interesting statistic in a survey. After surveying over 2,000 disabled individuals and their advocates, we found that the greatest barrier to independent living was "lack of self-confidence" (along with lack of transportation). This implies that it is not the lack of resources that is the major problem, but it is the lack of confidence and assertiveness in using these resources constructively and to one's benefit. Time and time again I have attended national conferences and heard many professionals voice in frustration over how they have developed and improved resources, making them barrier-free and totally accessible, and yet they are still unused. It almost sounded as if it was a general consensus that many disabled people, perhaps, expect resources just to cross into their field of vision and come knocking on their doors at home and making offers of their services. I am not implying that there are adequate and sufficient resources to meet all the needs of the disabled, and there certainly is tremendous room for growth in this area, but this growth will not come until the consumers acquire more confidence in their ability not only to utilize and cultivate resources, but to develop them as well. To illustrate this point even more clearly, compare the difference between two spinal cord injured clients using the services of the same agency. One disabled individual (consumer) is empowered and has an internal locus of control and thus acquires all of the benefits of that organization, whereas the other is dependent, timid (perhaps even unconsciously so as in the case of the overcompensator); thus, acquires little help from the agency. The role of the agency is to provide goods and services that facilitate a disabled individual's ability to live more independently and to meet his own needs. I emphasize the word facilitate, this does not mean to take care of. These agencies provide opportunities. It is the responsibility of the consumer to insure that these opportunities are actualized to the maximum extent possible. Often these agencies are staffed by professionals who serve as advocates, or other people in the community serve as advocates to assist with these agencies, but the best advocate for the disabled individual is himself. There is no substitute for self-advocacy and, in essence, this is what empowerment and this book is all about. To this end, I encourage you to explore these resources, but to do so with a sense of empowerment, and remember, empowerment means not only fulfilling your own needs, but respecting the needs of others as well. Thus, formal and informal relationships with representatives of these other entities should be cultivated to the maximum extent possible with nonthreatening, friendly assertiveness, similar to cultivating any relationship you would like to develop which we have discussed previously. To this end, with respect to setting goals in the "love and belonging" need domain, I will present these resources in appendices.

Chapter Seven

Solution Focused Exercises—Just Do It

"...Passion, you see, can be destroyed by a doctor. It cannot be created..."

Equus by Peter Shaffer

Let us try some exercises to get all of these concepts into motion, that is into action. Go back to the time when you became disabled. If you were born with a disability, go back to the time when you became aware of your disability, whenever that was. Or, if you were diagnosed with a disabling condition later in life, go back to the time when you became aware of that diagnosis. Now, think of each of the psychosocial needs—1) fun, 2) freedom 3) self-worth, and 4) love and belonging. Now, under each of the four needs, list all of the things you did or all of the activities in which you participated or any in which you met each need prior to your disabling condition. For example, under fun you may list skiing, reading books, having parties, jogging, being with friends or people you cared about, etc. It doesn't matter what it is. All that matters is that you experience fun and enjoyment during the activity. Notice also that you can put some activities in more than one column. For example, you can put skiing under the column for fun if it brought enjoyment to you, and you can list it under self-worth if it provided you with a sense of mastery, and you can even list it under love and belonging if it is an activity that brought you in contact with a social group such as a ski club. If this is the case, prioritize by the multiple listings according to their significance to you. For example, if skiing is most important as a source of self-worth, assign a number "1" to that entry of the activity, if it is secondly most important as fun assign a "2," and if lastly, it meets the need for love and belonging assign a "3." After you have listed all the circumstances and activities that brought you a sense of satisfaction with respect to your psychosocial needs, take a look at these lists. Are there too few or perhaps even none in one column, or are too few activities or only one or two activities fulfilling too many of your needs? Be honest with yourself in this examination. It's likely that you had greater psychosocial maturation, greater interdependence in meeting your psychosocial needs or greater internal locus of control if you have more things listed under each need. Take into consideration that developing activities and circumstances comes with time and it would be appropriate that you would have fewer activities listed if you acquired your disability at the age of ten as opposed to acquiring it at the age of thirty.

Now take a look at one of the lists and notice the activities. Examine them with respect to your internal locus of control, that is, the control you had over meeting these needs. For example, if you listed ice skating, reading, skiing, being with friends as activities for fun, keep in mind that it was not necessary for you to be an ice skater of Olympic caliber, simply that you pursued the activity of ice skating for fun. Whether or not you have the ability to be an Olympic skater is out of your control (basically, although this is probably somewhat debatable to a degree), but the ability to pursue skating as a fun or enjoyable activity is within your control, as long as skating really is fun and only you know that. Look at your lists under love

116

and belonging. What activities or relationships satisfy this need? Perhaps it is a relationship with your parents or a close friend, and perhaps it is membership in a social club. Regardless, whether the outcome of the relationship or the outcome of joining the social club was enjoyable is basically not within your control because it also involves the participation of other people, but if you enter and join those relationships in a positive manner and relate lovingly, positively, and supportingly, that is within your internal locus of control and will more likely result in more satisfactory relationships. That is, there is no guarantee that a relationship will be satisfactory regardless of your positive participation, but there is a guarantee that if you participate in a relationship negatively that it will be a negative outcome. The same with self-worth. What activities did you list there—perhaps pursuing a career or going to school or mastering a skill? Again, you may pursue that career and perhaps not make a million dollars or become a bank president, but you can still pursue it with all of our enthusiasm and potential and still feel good about yourself for what you have done. That is within your internal locus of control.

Now, consider each circumstance or activity on that list. Relive and re-experience the process that you had to go through. If you listed swimming, skiing, or riding your bike for fun, remember the first time you put on skis or went into the water. Do you remember the fear and the apprehension? Do you remember what you did in spite of it? Do you remember the positive neuro-associations you made with that fear, that it was okay to be afraid, that it was appropriate and this was only welcoming the challenge, and you didn't let it overwhelm you and beat you down? Do you remember the support you gave yourself and solicited from others despite that fear? Now, think about the mental and physical pain you had to go through, that is, the stress to learn each task. Remember falling off the bike and perhaps scraping your shin or elbows and the hurt? Do you remember it was probably embarrassing because you weren't learning to ride as quickly as some others? Do you remember wondering if your parents or friends were criticizing you for not doing what they wanted you to do? All of these painful and stressful situations must have had positive *neuro-associations* in order to master the task.

Now, create four new headings to develop four new lists with each psychosocial need being the heading for the list. Again, consider all the time back in your past up to the point where you became disabled or became aware of your disability. Think about all the activities and circumstances that you considered to meet each need but deferred or declined that activity and decided against it. For example, think about when you were fantasizing or considering taking up horseback riding, but declined to do so. Or, think about a special girl or guy you wanted so badly to call up, but decided against it, or the club you wanted to join, or the curriculum you wished to pursue, or the travels you wish to take, but with them all decided against it. This time, think about when encountering the fear, how you withdrew or fled, mentally and/or behaviorally, from the pursuit of this activity. By the way, I don't want to spend too much time dwelling on this because I don't want to get too caught up in past negative behaviors, but simply want to give a clear idea of how the dynamic works. Now, consider each one. Did you withdraw from this pursuit because it was simply too fearful or because, in your wise estimation, it was not obtainable? For example, if you decided against the activity of horseback riding, did you decline because you were too scared or because there was simply no way that you would be able to learn it realistically, probably because you didn't have enough money or, after having consulted someone, faced the fact that you didn't possess the physical requirements for horseback riding. Or, in the case of pursuing a date, did you abandon that pursuit because you were too fearful or made a realistic appraisal that the date would not have been obtainable because the person was going steady or engaged to someone else? In looking at some of these situations, it is crucial to be honest. It's okay to be honest here because you are doing this privately and no one is judging or evaluating you. Those activities you withdrew from because of fear, mark with an "F," and those you withdrew from because they were simply unobtainable, mark with a "U." Now look at those you marked with an "F." Do you remember what you had to do to be able to deal with the fear and the pain of the situation? For example, if you decided against horseback riding because it seemed to be too scary in any of its aspects, what defense did you use to manage this fear? Did you deny to yourself that it really was scary, or did you rationalize that it wasn't an important activity anyway? In doing so, you gave a positive neuro-association with a negative state, that is, a negative condition of not meeting the psychosocial needs. You can even create a list of activities that you tried but discarded prematurely. Again, use the example of horseback riding. You may have attempted the sport, but approached the fear with another defense mechanism such as overcompensation and set up grandiose expectations that you had to be the state champion or an Olympic horseback rider within the next two years and thus, inevitably became disappointed and gave it up. The same can happen with a relationship for the need of love and belonging. You can initially attempt a relationship, and approach the fear of rejection by terminating the relationship prematurely or approach the fear of intimacy by setting up grandiose expectations about the relationships and discarding it when these inflated expectations are not met. In these states of premature termination, you are making positive *neuro-associations* with these activities. That is, you are giving a pleasurable *neuro-association* to abandoning the sport of horseback riding because it is too painful to pursue (because you cannot become an Olympic gold medalist), or you can give a positive *neuro-association* to a pleasurable state of abandoning a relationship that is too painful, avoiding the fear and pain of rejection and/or intimacy.

* * * * * * *

"How can we get a man on the moon if he's unable to do things when he gets there? We have to come up with a solution."

Moon Shot, by Alan Shepard

Now, look at those activities or circumstances you avoided out of fear. Imagine what could have resulted if you had shifted your physical and mental state, that is, recreated a new and empowerment reframing. Rather than approaching the idea of horseback riding in a fearful physical state, that is, body tensed, shallow breathing, constricted muscles and slow, lethargic movements, you could have shifted your physical state into rapid and energetic movements signifying enthusiasm, deep rhythmic breathing and muscles feeling vibrant and positioned for activities. One of the major things about shifting the physical focus or physical state is that it breaks the vicious circle. When we become frightened by something and our bodies respond negatively, this increases the negative thinking and the negative physical state. For example, if we become frightened by a thought, our breathing can become shallow and rapid, but if we shift our breathing to full, energetic breathing, our thoughts can be reframed positively as well as our physical state. Breathing is crucially important because it is the one activity of the ANS (Autonomic Nervous System) that can easily become conscious as well as unconscious. This is not true, for example, with the muscles that line the blood vessels or the muscles of the heart which act more involuntarily and out of conscious control. But even with these muscles we can change them in their activity, not in the manner which we do our voluntary muscles like our arms and legs, but by relaxing them simply by focusing on them.

Now, let's go back to these needs fulfillment activities which we avoided because of fear. In addition to shifting our physical state, think about how the outcome might have been different if we shifted our mental focus. This is in reference to the empowerment reframing. In approaching the horseback riding, in addition to physically vitalizing our bodies, we could also have had a different mental focus. We could have made the positive *neuro-association* with the fear and the pain associated with learning the task. We could focus mentally and have a more realistic expectation, that is, bringing the task within our internal focus of control and simply pursuing it because it will provide us with means of enjoyment or self-worth, rather than hoping to become Olympic athletes or state champions. We could mentally focus on all the positive and beautiful things that will occur during the process of learning, such as meeting new people, being in the beautiful outdoors and in a natural environment, riding on a beautiful animal, and the works. We could even mentally refocus into an empowerment reframing by changing our values and belief systems. The belief system is simply a set of ideas you have about a certain circumstance or activity. For example, you could have a belief system that is negative, unconsciously or consciously, with respect to horseback riding such as that people who ride horses are unsophisticated country people or snobs. These types of belief systems are limiting and usually are in response to fear and reinforce the fear.

Now let's jump to the present. I really didn't want to spend too much time focusing on problem-saturated situations of the past. Remember, the process of empowerment is realizing that change is always possible regardless of the past. The past in no way equals or reflects the future, and if we stay problem focused by focusing on the problems in the past, we lose sight of solutions. Empowerment reframing is essentially that we become solution focused rather than problem focused. The solutions are in some way found by giving positive neuro-associations with growth and independent ability in meeting our psychosocial needs more flexibly and in a broader variety of ways. That is, a solution exists when we give a positive *neuro-association* to the fear and pain that is associated in moving in a positive direction. Likewise, a solution exists when we give a negative *neuro-association* to the absence of fear and pain in moving in a negative direction towards the deprivation and denial of activities that meet these needs.

Now, let us consider the point in your life when you became disabled or aware of your disability. Again, make four columns with four headings, one for each psychosocial need—fun, freedom, self-worth, and love and belonging. What activities or circumstances do you undertake to meet each of these needs? It doesn't matter how insignificant or significant they, but list any activity or circumstance that meets each of the needs, and again, you may list one activity under several columns. Prioritize these by assigning a number to that need is most significantly met by that activity. For example, if skiing is the activity that fulfills the need for both fun and self-worth, but fun is the more important need, assign a number "1" to that. Now here is an important point. It doesn't matter if you believe that the activity is positive or negative, that is, healthy or unhealthy. You may list eating for fun and might want to break that down a bit more such as eating sweets, or you may list using alcohol for having fun or meeting one of your other needs such as self-worth, intimacy, or freedom (alcohol plays a role in all of these needs). Also, as an extreme example, you may list being controlling or even abusive to your partner or spouse as an activity you use to feel self-worth, or love and belonging. Try to remember that any behavior or activity you do in life has meaning and that can include an activity you conventionally think of as not doing. For example, you may think of staying home as not being an activity but in fact, staying home and isolating yourself is an activity. Think of all the things that you do and try to categorize them under one of the psychosocial needs, or more of them if necessary. Now, next to each activity under each need column, make an honest appraisal if you believe that activity to be healthy or unhealthy. There is a general rule that an activity is most likely unhealthy if it is interfering with your physical and/or psychological growth or is interfering with anyone else's physical

122

or psychological growth. This task may be a bit tricky but try anyway. You may wonder for example if eating sweets is healthy or unhealthy, and again as a general rule, it will most likely not be unhealthy if you don't do it too often and you have a lot of other options for meeting your need for fun; whereas if it is only one or two of the activities you do for enjoyment and fun, it most likely will be unhealthy. That is, overeating sweets could be destructive to your physical growth and an indicator of social isolation and other psychosocial needs deprivation. Take a careful look at these lists. How do they strike you? Does there seem to be ample opportunity and activities for meeting your needs healthfully or is it too restrictive, indicating needs deprivation. For example, if you listed watching TV as a source of enjoyment, is that the only one or only one out of a few activities and perhaps an indicator of lack of fun and lack or other activities?

Now, let's create four new lists, once again creating four headings, one each for fun, freedom, self-worth and love and belonging. Think about all of the activities and circumstances, occurring after your disability, which you considered but declined or withdrew from. List these under each heading and, again, be honest. Did you consider going back to school but declined or did you consider taking up skiing again but decided against it? Did you consider becoming more socially active and mingle more with people but held back or even refused when there were golden opportunities? Did you consider learning Braille to meet your need for fun and self-worth but decided against it? For your need for freedom, did you consider traveling by yourself once or cultivating a relationship in which you could express yourself freely and honestly (remember, freedom does not necessarily mean being alone, but expressing yourself as an individual). Now, again without taking too much time because we don't want to focus on problems, look at each activity under the columns. Again, being as honest as possible, mark each activity that you withdrew from because of overexcessive fear with an "F" and the other activities you withdrew from simply because they were realistically unobtainable with a "U." (This is similar to what we previously did by labeling activities healthy or unhealthy.) Being honest is crucial here. For example, if you identified skiing as an activity you avoided, you may have initially believed it to be because it was unobtainable, but in reality you did have the money to afford it, could have gotten to a mountain with a friend or family member, found someone to teach you adaptive skiing, etc. By the way, I am not implying that simply because an activity is possible that it should have been pursued. Sometimes activities are possible but are rejected simply because of time management problems or other practical problems with respect to appraising overall benefits. Now, looking at those activities you have identified with an "F," think about how the response could have been different if you had shifted your physical and mental focus to positive, empowerment reframing. Rather than considering the possibility of skiing with a weakened, intimidated physical state characterized by anxiety, rapid, shallow breathing and tense muscles along with a negative mental focus, we adopt an empowerment reframing position and make positive neuro-associations with the stress of learning to ski by making our physical state positive and positively shifting our mental focus. That is, we look at, despite the fear, pain and stress of learning it, the positive things skiing could and most likely will bring to us—being in the fresh open air in the beautiful mountains, being with other people, doing something that is a healthy, physical outlet from our mental stresses. Shifting the mental focus positively could also mean shifting the belief system such as "people who ski are rich snobs" to "everyone has something positive within him or her or about him or her." Now a good way to determine whether we avoided a particular activity out of fear or simply because it was unobtainable is to consider whether we would have pursued this activity even if we had approached it with a positive empowerment approach. In other words, you are positive with your mental focus and your physical state is positive in approaching the idea of skiing but simply decide it is too expensive (considering other areas you want to prioritize your money in) or impractical with respect to time.

Now we are going to come to an important activity, an activity that is now going to become future oriented. What we have been doing is looking at how, both prior to and after the disabling condition, we have attempted to meet our psychosocial needs. But now we are going to come to the important task of goal setting with respect to these needs, a future directed activity of crucial importance. A brief discussion of goal setting will be helpful here. Goal setting has always been a major part of my clinical work with clients. Providing clearly defined, specific goals lays a clear groundwork for what we are focusing upon and thus leads to clearer solutions to the problems or situations that are necessary to solve in order to achieve the goals. Studies have been done that demonstrate that clear and specific articulation and identification of goals lead to more positive outcome results. With respect to the solution-focused problem solving we had discussed earlier, goal setting is the activity that moves us into the preparation, or positioning, stage that prepares us for action and change. Now I would like you to do several things. First, I would like you to just list at random all the things you would like to accomplish, regardless of the time it takes to accomplish them. Take some time to do this. They may seem like major things or minor things, but what is important is that they feel subjectively important to you. You may think of wanting to achieve a possible career, a new skill, travel, or find some new way to be able to cope better with your disability. Just list them randomly and as free flowingly as possible. Try not to think too much about them, certainly do not think about whether they are possible or not. Just list them, and give yourself time to do this. After that task has been completed, I would like you to take a look at the list and identify which psychosocial need each particular goal addresses. For example, if you listed something like learning how to ski, you may want to identify that primarily with the need for fun and perhaps secondarily with the need for self-worth. If you identify more than one need that an activity represents, prioritize the importance of the needs they represent. Now I would like you to make four headings with columns. These would be labeled fun, freedom, self-worth, and love and belonging. Then list your goals under the appropriate column. Again, if you picked one goal that meets three needs, make sure it has some numerical priority assigned to it and perhaps a higher position on the lists. Now, using these four lists, try to more fully develop these lists by thinking of other goals within each psychosocial need domain. Again, during this, you do not want to hold anything back with your intellect, let your emotions run freely. The intellect will come later. As a matter of fact, it might be a good idea to think back when you were a child to things you fantasized or daydreamed about or even to some of the things you fantasize and daydream about currently. Take time to do this, but it should be done in a time limited manner where you have full opportunity for concentration without distraction.

What we are doing here is not only projecting into the future with clear, specific objectives, but we are creating a sense of positive stress, that is, differentiation between what exists now and what you expect to exist in the future. In doing this you are creating a set of "greater expectations" which you can internalize into your whole being and begin to develop positive *neuro-associations* with respect to the state of your physical being and your mental being in the perceptions of these goals.

Now that you have these rather random comprehensive lists of goals by category, let's look at each goal one by one. Which ones are goals that you feel energized by, turned on by? That is, if you had this goal achieved would you feel truly alive, not just from the avoidance of pain but truly and pleasurably feeling like you're enjoying your life. What we are doing here is separating the goals that are more oriented to the absence of pain rather than those that are oriented to the acquisition of pleasure. Remember, most human behavior is oriented towards the absence of pain rather than the acquisition of pleasure. So if you have a goal under fun and enjoyment such as watching TV, but come to consider that is not something you really wish to accomplish other than it is a way to fill up blank spaces in your life, you may not rate this too highly. On the other hand, say you have established a goal like learning how to ski or horseback ride. As you think about accomplishing this goal the vitality which the thought provides suggests a higher ranking. But, remember, the important thing is how you project yourself to actually feel. These are your subjective feelings and no one else's. You may want to establish a ranking system from one to five. A numerical rank of one or two would suggest that the goal is associated with the absence of pain while a numerical ranking of four or five would suggest that the goal is associated with the acquisition of pleasure. A numerical ranking of three would mean that you are uncertain as to whether a goal avoids pain or provides pleasure.

Chapter Eight
The Characteristics of Empowered People

"However, submission is not the only way of avoiding aloneness and anxiety. The other way, the only one which is productive and does not end in an insoluble conflict, is that of *spontaneous relationship to man and nature*, a relationship that connects the individual with the world without eliminating his individuality. This kind of relationship—the foremost expressions of which are love and productive work—are rooted in the integration and strength of the total personality and are therefore subject to the very limits that exist for the growth of the self."

Escape From Freedom by Erich Fromm

Now that we have finished discussing the process of empowerment, let's talk about the end result. What do empowered people look like? What are there characteristics? How do they feel, think and behave? What are their habitual patterns of behavior? In my view these are the essential characteristics of personal empowerment:

1. *Empowered people are self-aware and, more importantly, self accepting.* Individuals who are empowered have a good grasp of who they are, what they are, how they value things and the like. They are honest in this appraisal, recognizing all aspects of themselves including their limits and strengths. They do not judge these limits with themselves, as they do not with other people, because they realize this negativism will get in the way of their own growth. They accept all aspects of themselves just as they do with others because they fundamentally realize, given certain social and psychological circumstances, they are doing the best they can. It is a fundamental belief of self-acceptance and this leads to acceptance of others, regardless of where one "is at" in life.

2. *Empowered people take responsibility.* Individuals who are personally empowered take responsibility of their own feelings, thoughts and behaviors. They take responsibility for their perceptions, how they view the world. Empowered individuals do not blame other individuals or groups of individuals for their predicaments and situations. While they may recognize the influences and encouragement of other people, empowered individuals know that they always have a choice of how they are going to respond to any given situation. That's exactly what responsibility means, ability to respond, the word originally derived from the French word, *respondere*, which simply means "to look at." You look at any given situation and make the choice about how you are going to respond. And that choice influences the outcome. For example, individuals who are more into power, control or manipulation usually respond to other people's criticism by automatically becoming angry, defensive and critical in return, whereas, empowered individuals usually respond to criticism in a manner that reflects responsibility. In other words, they choose to see that the critical individual is in some way an immature person, and do not take the criticism personally or personalize it, and thus, usually respond in a manner that would somehow bring the situation to a more positive resolution. Empowered people take responsibility for the choices and the responses

130

they make to the world around them without blaming the world for where they're "at," because, no matter where they are at, they always have the choice to focus positively on their situation. (Remember the miracle question we discussed in the last chapter.)

3. *Empowered people set goals.* Goal setting means short-term as well as long-term goals. Empowered individuals have a clear picture of where they want to be with their lives, set the interim goals or objectives which are necessary to meet the long-range goals, and use this picture as a leading force in their lives. This goal setting is a mission statement upon which their lives are built. Thus, empowered individuals are pro-active rather than reactive, reacting to influence and pressures from the world around them in getting them sidetracked. Furthermore, these goals are established from an internal locus of control, something that really excites them, turns them on, gives them a sense of meaningfulness in their lives. Often, in my counseling practice, I use imagery to help people visualize themselves in an ideal situation and then try to help them imagine exactly where they want to be and under what circumstances. This is so they can come to make a more pro-active decision in the real world situation as to what they would like their lives to be like, even if this is ideal. Occasionally I will do regressive work, in going back to the past, in which they can recall childhood, adolescence, or earlier experiences in which they had a real desire for something, that was extinguished as a result of family or social pressures. Of course, goal setting with respect to empowered people does not only involve a high level of interest, but an adequate amount of ability as well. It is from these ideals (interests and abilities) that empowered people decide what goals to have. For example, as mentioned earlier, an empowered individual may really love athletics but may not have the ability to become a professional athlete. She could develop a career in some related field such as a sports broadcaster or even an attendant at a sports arena, or a statistician. This adaptability goes hand in hand with self-awareness (see characteristic #1) and it is crucial for empowered individuals.

4. *Empowered individuals focus on solutions*. The empowered individual reaches the previously mentioned goals in a solution focused manner as we have discussed in this book. This is in essence the most effective management of time and skills possible to reach the goals that have been previously established. Again, about 20% of the time is spent on assessing the problem and 80% of the time is spent on researching and focusing on solutions. Twenty percent focus on the problem is required in order to clarify and assess it in the most positive manner, despite the frustration level of the problem and is actually part of the solution process. Empowered people focus primarily on those problems that relate to their goals in life, not on problems that are relatively unimportant to their goals or their mission statements. Interestingly, they seek solutions which support a high level of empowerment so that a positive frame of reference from an internal locus of control is maintained. The solution is derived from what they have control over. They ask the "miracle question": What would be different if the problem disappeared overnight? For example, we do not have control over getting the job that we really want because that decision is made by another person, an employer. But we do have control over doing everything we possibly can to get that job. And, even if we don't get the job, we ask ourselves what would be different if the problem (not having the job) were not a problem. We would be happier, still working positively on relationships that are important to us, still maintaining a high level of self-worth and exploring opportunities for our freedom. By pursuing these activities within our control, we maximize the chances of getting the job or having other positive options because our levels of frustration are decreased.

5. *Empowered individuals are cooperative and collaborative, not competitive, in their relationships*. Empowered individuals do not compare themselves to other individuals for their self-worth, or their self-validation simply because they have an internal locus of control and get all the validation they need from themselves. Thus, they

do not have to think of themselves as being better than other individuals or being competitive with them in winning in arguments because they realize that one of them must be a loser. Empowered people value other people's empowerment and simply do not desire others to be losers, do not look at viewpoints as right or wrong, think that every viewpoint, regardless of how different, is valid, and thus, every viewpoint is "right" from the value perspectives, their histories, their perceptions and so forth. Personal viewpoints are a basic human right which relates to human dignity. Thus, empowered individuals are not competitive, they are collaborative and when an inevitable conflict arises they do not try to change the other individual to conform to their own point of view, but find a way to negotiate or compromise in which each individual gets what he or she wants, and if that is not possible, they positively agree to disagree and search for cooperation elsewhere while still regarding the person on the other end of the conflicting issue in a positive manner. Thus, empowered individuals are able to separate issues and individuals' behaviors from the individuals themselves. Although empowered individuals accept and respect different points of view, they do not respect and condone behaviors that are intrusive to the rights and needs of others simply because they value empowerment for everyone.

6. *Empowered individuals empathize in their communication.* Empowered individuals try to understand, then to be understood. Accordingly, in their intimate relationships, whether developed or in the process of development, they strive to love before being loved. This is perhaps the most important quality of the empowered individual. This is where the art of listening and healthy, mature communication patterns come in. Empathy is perhaps the most powerful quality in a human relationship. It is the art in which we strive to understand another person by projecting ourselves into that person's consciousness and understanding how that person is thinking, feeling and behaving, even if you do not agree with it. It is a quality that

133

empowered individuals have that enables them to realize that just about every person on this planet, regardless of his level of immaturity and even destructiveness, is, in essence, doing the best he can. His feelings, thoughts and behaviors make sense in terms of where he is coming from, even if his values are diametrically opposed to that of empowered individuals. Think of it this way, suppose you encounter an individual who is quite self-destructive, even homicidal, and when that individual is asked why he is homicidal or to explain why he is so angry, the homicidal person may report that because of the way he was raised as a child he believes that the whole world is against him and he better eliminate people rather than let them eliminate him. While this certainly does not give any justification for his totally inexcusable behavior, just listening in an empathic manner will inevitably reduce the homicidal individual's level of suspicion simply because here is an individual that truly wants to understand where he is coming from. This is where we get into the situation where we often hear, "You can't possibly understand what it is like to not have your sight or go through a divorce" (possibly even if the listener is blind or divorced himself). The empowered listener most likely would respond, "You're right, I don't know what it is like for you to be blind or divorced, so please tell me so I can understand." Again, this is not to imply that empowered individuals condone or tolerate destructive behavior because, as I mentioned in Characteristic 2, empowered people believe in responsibility, individuals have to take responsibility for their behaviors, including those behaviors that interfere with the rights and empowerment needs of other individuals.

7. *Empowered individuals are genuine in their relationships.* Empowered individuals are open and honest in their relationships, especially in their intimate relationships, or relationships they are cultivating towards intimacy. A simple reason for this is because of the empowered individual's internal locus of control, he doesn't particularly care about how another individual regards him or her simply because he validates himself. The empowered individual doesn't

have to prove anything to anyone, nor does he seek other people's approval. In part, this characteristic leads to a greater sense of community since his lack of competitiveness avoids the "bottomless pit syndrome" which says you are not good enough unless you are at the top. It is this characteristic, along with Characteristic 5 (lack of competitiveness), that enables empowered individuals to believe that they don't necessarily have to be the best, they can simply be better at what they are. It is the lack of these characteristics which account for such personal tragedies as John Belushi, Jim Morrison and others who were so driven to be the best in the eyes of others, particularly as reflected in the media. The interesting thing about being more open and honest in relationships, including acknowledging limits, is that it encourages openness and honesty in other individuals, thus relationships have a more relaxed atmosphere. This empowerment characteristic sets a better basis for establishing Characteristic 6—empathy through understanding—simply because you cannot feel understood if you are not being honest. You are being controlling and manipulative to get the desired response from the other individual. The goal is not to be understood, but rather to manipulate. Sounds too easy, doesn't it?

8. *Empowered individuals are always striving for their physical, mental, spiritual and psychosocial growth.* Empowered individuals realize the significance of their needs, including physical, spiritual and psychosocial (emotional, mental and social). Empowered individuals strive for the physical growth through appropriate physical exercise (especially aerobic exercise) not only because it supports the other three dimensions, but increases significantly the chances for a longer life in which to live in an empowering manner. Interestingly, it is the awareness of death and coming to terms with it that enables us to truly live and this is why cultivating a spiritual self is so important as well. Finding ways to grow in these four dimensions enables us to expand our repertoire of choices for fulfilling all of our needs, especially your psychosocial needs which are directly associated with a personal sense of empowerment. Again, to grow means

135

doing new things, which involves taking risks, accepting humility and passing through awkward periods of time. Some of these new things we must do simply because we can no longer do the old things, and meet our needs through the old ways. The reason it is so necessary for growth in these dimensions is because it helps us to deal with inevitable losses in life. A man who has only one activity for fun, such as marathon running, is headed for trouble in the aging process when that is no longer possible unless he has an empowering attitude and is willing to cultivate new activities. The greater the experience at trying new things for either replacing old losses or simply adding to existing options, the greater the individual's ability to grow by letting go of old options that are no longer possible rather than letting go of life. In my view, what is particularly helpful in growing in these four dimensions is teaching it, whether as a teacher in a formal or informal relationship, or as a therapist. Teaching is helpful because it not only reaffirms our position which embraces the value of growth and personal empowerment, but it also sharpens our focus in pursuing an empowered life. (This is a major part of my motivation for writing this book.) We must be careful that in the process of teaching in whatever form, we are not pressuring or trying to change people. The simple reasons for this is that empowerment embodies the sacred value of responsibility which primarily means choosing a response and, if we are pressuring, we are discouraging people's dignity and their ability to choose. The effective teaching of the empowerment mode, the process of empowerment is explained and clarified as an option which includes the benefits they can be expected to acquire and simply allowing the individual the right to make an informed choice while simultaneously respecting where the other individual is at including his thoughts, feelings, behaviors and value systems. Empowered people understand that pressuring and trying to change people is likely to be counterproductive.

Let's Turn America Around by Changing,
Nope Not the Government, Nope Not Big Business,
But By Changing You

"...My fellow Americans, ask not what your country can do for you, but what you can do for your country."
President John F. Kennedy

"...It is essential to understand that the very principle of Nazism is its radical opportunism. What mattered was to hundreds of thousands of petit bourgeoisie who in the normal course of development had little chance to gain money or power as members of the Nazi bureaucracy who now got a large part of the wealth and prestige they forced the upper classes to share with them. Other members who were not members of the Nazi machine were given the jobs taken away from the Jews and political enemies. And for the rest, although they did not get bread, they got 'circuses.' The emotional satisfaction afforded by these sadistic spectacles and by an ideology (Nazism)...was able to compensate them for a time at least for the fact that their lives had been impoverished economically and culturally (and psychologically)."
Escape From Freedom by Erich Fromm

"In how many years can some people exist
before they're allowed to be free."
"Yes, and how many times can a man turn
his head and pretend that he just doesn't see."
Blowin' in the Wind by Bob Dylan

I truly believe that the roots of the major problems in America are the lack of empowered people in our society on a national, state-wide and community level. Empowered individuals are independent, or more significantly interdependent, as individuals are thus look more for opportunity programs in this country rather than "take-care-of-me" programs. Because empowered individuals are interdependent and take full responsibility for meeting their own basic needs, physically and psychosocially, they do the best possible job they can to bet the job that meets these requirements. If such jobs do not exist, they do the best possible job on an individual or self-employment basis, to meet that requirement. If neither possibility seems to exist, or the options for both choices are greatly diminished, they participate in activities which would undoubtedly contribute to an economy that would offer more in both arenas. Empowered individuals believe there are enough resources to go around which essentially means everyone in this country, under ideal circumstances, would have the means, monetarily and otherwise, to satisfy their physical and psychosocial needs for well-being. Furthermore, empowered individuals are not competitive and do not value themselves by comparison, or by being "better" than other individuals due to external social indexes such as wealth, social class, or job prestige. Rather, they value individuals who themselves are empowered and are able to take care of their physical and psychosocial needs interdependently and thus are more genuine in relationships. Therefore, they are likely to seek leaders with these same empowerment characteristics.

To understand this dynamic more fully, it is important to understand (even if oversimplified) the systemic interrelatedness of government, corporate business and consumers who are also voters. Consumers and voters who are not empowered, or disempowered, tend to look at the government in dependent ways and are more likely to look for entitlement programs, "take-care-of-me" programs, because in their view they assume the only means for contentment and happiness is to be given something, particularly money, without the pain of having to work for it. This is not a judgmental statement, but a simple recognition of the fact that for disempowered people to take care of their own physical and psychosocial needs interdependently seems insurmountable. Because disempowered people do not take responsibilities for their own lives, are not pro-active and do not strive towards goals interdependently, they fail to communicate effectively, they blame the government, big business and the overall economy for their plight and misery. Thus they tend to look to national leaders to remedy misery and promise to take care of their unhappiness by creating more jobs, entitlement programs and health care systems that are treatment oriented rather than prevention oriented. This creates an impossible situation for the politician if he or she wants to get elected and needs the votes of the consumer. In turn, the politicians, as potentially elected public servants, are also disempowered and esteem themselves by external locus of control standards of wealth and power and thus do not communicate genuinely with the grassroots consumers and sincerely explain to these people that the "take-care-of-me" programs that foster dependency costs the government too much money and plunges us into a staggering national debt which we all know about. Rather than sharing this truthful staggering reality to the voter and encouraging him or her to find better ways to take care of him/herself, the politicians make promises to the contrary in order to get the vote.

Furthermore, the leaders on a local, statewide and national level must turn to the big businesses and corporate executives to get the funding necessary to manage the grossly expensive political campaigns. Leaders and lobbyists for big business, including CEOs, tend to be disempowered in their constant struggle to be on the top, falling into the "bottomless pit syndrome," striving to be all powerful through the acquisition of more wealth, social prestige and control which they can never get quite enough of since their locus of control is external, not internal. If their locus of control were internal and they were not driven with the all-consuming striving for power, money, and social control they would be able to take more direct responsibility for meeting their physical and psychosocial needs rather economically, simply because it does not require a huge amount of money to meet their needs interdependently. Does it really require a seven- and even an eight-figure salary to be content in this world, to be an empowered individual who not only has a strong pro-active, goal setting character, but is also relating to other individuals genuinely and lovingly? I heard a recent report that CEOs in this country by 1992 were making 225 times the salary of the average working individual. You not only have to wonder why all that money is necessary, but how driven the top corporate executives must be to either get to the top or stay on top. I often feel more compassion for these individuals than the common, struggling working individual since this individual has to be operating on a treadmill of frustration. The definition of frustration is: the closer to the goal you become, yet do not quite obtain it, the more frustrated you become and if the goal is to be the most powerful person, by external standards in the country or the world (which is an impossible goal), then this individual has to be extremely frustrated. Yet these are the corporate executives and business leaders who sustain not only the status quo, but the possibility of greater wealth by pouring money into campaigns where the politicians promise, usually secretly, to support their disempowered positions. Simultaneously, these public officials, actually public servants, are making campaign promises for better "take-care-of-me" entitlement programs or at least middle class tax breaks, a promise they know is impossible to fulfill on a balanced budget basis, but a promise they must make, nevertheless, to get the vote. Once a public official is elected and inevitably is unable to fulfill that promise, he typically blames something or someone else, usually the competitive political party, for his inability to meet the campaign promises.

In my view, the real culprit in this system is the disempowered consumer and voter. If consumers and voters were more responsible for meeting their own needs without depending on external forces such as government and big business to meet their needs interdependently, they would be looking more to officials who promise not "take-care-of-me" dependent programs, but programs that foster and encourage interdependence such as education, employment training, on-the-job training and rehabilitation programs. This in turn would force a greater supply of potential leaders who would run on that platform, diminish the supply of potential leaders who would support the special interests of big business leaders, lobbyists and CEOs. Ultimately, due to the changing national consciousness of empowerment, big business leaders and corporate officials would change their own agendas from one of power with external control and manipulation to one of genuine empowerment since this is what the grassroots population is validating.

While I do believe there is a legitimate and valid place for entitlement programs for individuals, particularly dependent children who are not able to earn a decent living through their own resources, I simultaneously believe that everybody can be making a contribution. Mothers on welfare are unable to join the labor force or find a job, not only because of unavailable jobs but because of the needs of their young children. There are many individuals whose level of disability is so significant that it would most likely preclude any possibility of entering the labor force either on a competitive or supportive employment basis. Thus, the "take-care-of-me" programs would certainly be justified. However, I truly believe and, in fact, I can unequivocally say that I do know that there are many individuals in the nation's entitlement programs who could be making a greater contribution to their families, community and nation on some level, whether it be paid employment or volunteerism. They could more significantly enrich their feelings of self-worth, a feeling that they are making a difference, while fulfilling the other psychosocial needs as well, including a sense of belonging, fun and enjoyment, and creatively (the process of freedom). To give an example, I remember in the early days of establishing the nation's first program to provide professional counseling to disabled individuals on a community basis, systematic level, counseling for independent living, I needed help to read the monumental and massive amounts of material necessary for policy development as well as service implementation. I contacted nursing homes to find elderly individuals, some of them being depressed and idle, so that they could give me a hand with reading by reading into cassette tapes for me. I truly believe everyone can be doing more to enhance and strengthen communities and the nation, but not doing things in a disempowered, dependent and external locus of control manner, but rather doing more in an empowered, meaningful manner through the use of creativity and courage. Most mothers, if not all mothers, on welfare could be doing more to contribute while simultaneously enriching their lives and developing a stronger sense of community. And I certainly know from a personal as well as professional perspective this applies to most disabled individuals as well.

Lack of personal empowerment is also a fundamental dynamic that negatively impacts our health care system as well. Responding to life's challenges on a direct and empowered basis means that we are taking care of ourselves, all aspects of ourselves, certainly including physical as well as psychological. Health means strengthening, and strengthening means prevention rather than a treatment "take-care-of-me" approach. I have heard of estimates in the mid-80s that approximately 15% of the individuals enrolled in health care systems and insurance (private and public) are using up approximately 85% of the services. I have seen television reports about people who deliberately and intentionally make themselves ill so they will be hospitalized and cared for by professional caretakers in a desperate attempt to deal with loneliness and emptiness in their lives. A motivating drive behind this self-destructive force is the pursuit of dependent, submissive relationships which are symbiotic in a desperate attempt to acquire a security that only proves to be illusory and unreal. True security comes from within which, stated simply, is self-awareness, generally recognizing one's own limits as well as strengths that are continuously changing. True relationships, including love, are supportive, not symbiotic and support comes primarily from the empathic ability to listen and understand other people's limits and strengths rather than fixing up other people's weaknesses and competing with their strengths. Simply speaking, empowered individuals want to live to the fullest of their potential and have little interest in being taken care of and thus being sick.

Yet, the transition to an empowered life is just that, a transition, and can only occur if the transition comes from within from an internal locus of control and cannot be externally applied or socially pressured through social policy and the enforcing legal system. The laws of self-determination are crucial in the empowerment process and if a person chooses to live his or her life self-destructively, that still must be respected, as long as the destruction is not intrusive to others. We become a co-dependent, counterproductive society when we try to force change, even in the rationalizing that it is for the human good and dignity, if coercion, no matter how subtle, is applied. Thus, rather than forcing and mandating human growth and empowerment, we can encourage it in the most dynamic and effective manner possible. This can occur in several ways. Perhaps the most important is working on our own growth and empowerment. That is, not only serving as a role model, but also by affirming and validating other people's growth, creativity and love, while ignoring their stagnation, destructiveness and hate. School systems could perhaps contribute, as well as families, by teaching and enabling children to build self-esteem and communicate accordingly. Courses in professional programs could be offered and perhaps, in extreme cases, mandated for adults who are obviously and chronically stuck in entitlement programs and leading unproductive as well as socially isolated lives. This mandation would not be enough to change the individual, but would create a situation in which the individual is confronted with the possibility of growth while his or her fears are being supported. The real message here, however, is that the changing and renaissance of this country depends on each and every one of us taking responsibility for our lives and sense of well-being, and to the extent that this is collectively accomplished, there will be a naturally corresponding level of optimism, competence and productivity as the nation is launched into the twenty-first century.

"Ladies and Gentlemen:

We often hear politicians saying how they want government to empower you so that you can do things. 'That's not the way it is,' Ryan told them forcefully. 'Thomas Jefferson wrote that government derived their power from the consent of the governed, that's you.... Most of all, the government does not empower you. You empower the government. Ours is a government of the people. You are not people who belong to the government. Tomorrow, you will not be electing masters, you will be choosing employees, servants of your will, guardians of your rights. We do not tell you what to do, you tell us what to do. ...Government service may be an important duty and a great responsibility, but it is not supposed to be a blessing for those who serve. It is your government servants who are supposed to sacrifice for you, not you who sacrifice for them...

You and I know that not all government employees are like that. That is not their fault, that is your fault. If you do not demand the best, you will not get the best. If you do not give the right measure of power to the right kind of people, then the wrong people will take more power than they need and they will use it the way they want, not the way you want... America is (also) your child. America is a country forever young. America needs the right people to look after her. It is your job to pick the right people, regardless of party or race or gender, anything other than talent and integrity...God gave you a free will. The Constitution is there to protect your right to exercise that will. If you fail to exercise your will intelligently, them you have betrayed yourself, and neither I nor anyone else can fix that for you."

President Jack Ryan
Executive Orders by Tom Clancy

145

Appendix A

Resources that address the need for fun, recreation, sports, and enjoyment

Disabled Sports USA
451 Hungerford Drive, Suite 100
Rockville, MD 20850
(301) 217-0960
FAX: (301) 217-0968
TDD: (301) 217-0963

Comments: Formerly National Handicapped Sports and Recreational Association, Washington, DC. This organization provides international sport and recreational activities. There are also chapters throughout the country serving under this parent organization. For example, there is a New England Handicapped Sports Association (NEHSA) located at Mount Sunapee, New Hampshire. You can find out about a local chapter in your area by contacting the national organization listed above in Rockville, MD. Also, this organization should have much literature and other information about sporting and recreational activities provided by related organizations.

United Way

Comments: As you most likely know, United Way collects funds and supports helping agencies throughout the country. There should be a United Way agency in your area or at least one that serves your area. I am not talking about agencies that received United Way funds and are designated as United Way affiliates; I am referring to the United Way itself. They also publish a directory which lists agencies not only alphabetically, but categorizes them by function such as recreational agencies and disabled organizations. This resource would not only be helpful for recreational activities, but the other domains as well and I will list it here only for convenience. The directory costs around $25.00, but you should be able to have it available at your local library, or you could call your local United Way agency to find out how else the directory might be available without cost if that is desired. Also remember, libraries are to be covered under the ADA and are supposed to make materials and their services accessible to the disabled. This will be explained in a later (the ADA) section.

Blind Outdoor Leisure Development (BOLD)

Comments: There are many BOLD programs which seem to provide mainly skiing and other outdoor activities for individuals who are blind and other disabled individuals. I know there is one at Aspen Mountain, Colorado and Loon Mountain, Lincoln, New Hampshire and they, most likely, can provide you with the names of other BOLD programs, perhaps one in your area. They usually provide ski instruction, lift tickets, and other accommodations at no cost or greatly reduced costs. Also, most mountains have a policy with respect to disabled skiing, sometimes offering ski lift rates at no cost and reduced costs. You would want to contact the region you are about to approach and if they don't have a policy they most likely will know of a nearby mountain that does.

Shake-A-Leg, Inc.
Miami, FL (305) 858-5550; Newport, RI (401) 849-8898

Comments: Located in Newport, RI and in Miami, FL. Provides a variety of leisure and recreational activities for the spinal cord injured as well as for those with other related disabilities. Sailing and other aquatic sports are their main activities.

YMCA, YWCA

Comments: You can look up your local agency in the telephone book. These agencies are nonprofit and often receive federal funds, mandating them to be accessible and nondiscriminatory to the disabled.

They primarily provide opportunities for all community members, disabled or otherwise. They also may have some specialized disabled activities. For example, the Arthritis Foundation has special aquatics programs at some local YMCAs.

American Water Ski Association
Florida (941) 324-4341
Comments: This organization is the official sanctioned body for water ski tournaments and relations for other water ski activities and has recently developed a disabled component which basically sponsors annual water ski tournaments and clinics for the disabled. They also have available regional AWSA chapters which may also include disabled water ski activities which could be located in your area.

American Blind Skiers Association
Santa Monica, California
Comments: This organization used to sponsor annual water ski competitions and clinics in Orlando, FL but is currently in a stage of transition due to the death of its founder and chairman, Ed Kanan. The Splash N' Ski School at Sonesta Village, Orlando, Florida which was contracted by American Blind Skiers Association to conduct its activities is still available and their proprietors, Ray and Jackie Sturgeon, are very knowledgeable and helpful with disabled water skiers.

Rehabilitation Services Administration (RSA)
U.S. Department of Education
Washington, DC
(202) 205-8206
Comments: The RSA which funds a variety of federal programs for the disabled (including statewide vocational rehabilitation) also has a program which funds recreational projects for individuals with severe disabilities. You may contact this federal office in order to

determine organizations that have been funded to provide recreational services. These programs funded by RSA for recreational projects are innovative and serve a wide variety of disabilities, but you may have to do a little research to determine the feasibility (including geographic location) of such recreational services for your needs. Your local vocational rehabilitation unit (Statewide Vocational Rehabilitation Agency) may be able to determine for you who is funded under these programs as well. Some information should also be accessible to you to accommodate your disability. For example, if you are blind, this information should be available on audio tape cassette.

Centers For Independent Living (CILs)
Washington, DC
(202) 889-5802

Comments: The above phone number is to obtain a directory of a CIL in your area. Basically, this center for independent living is a nonprofit organization that provides a wide range of services to individuals with a wide range of disabilities. To receive federal funds through the Rehabilitation Act, the organization must be governed by a board of directors that has a majority of disabled individuals. Typically, many of its staff members are also disabled or strong advocates of the disabled. They provide four core services: 1) independent living skills training (in one area or another); 2) peer support; 3) information and referral; and 4) advocacy. Some CILs may provide direct recreational services. They should have information through their information and referral component about recreational services for the disabled in your area or region. CILs should be considered for other activities in the other needs domain area to be outlined.

General Comments: The bottom line here is to be creative and aggressive in your research. Remember, every problem has a solution and, if a problem you are encountering is locating a resource to meet your needs, find the solution for that problem. Get into the empowerment mode. All movies, theaters, stadiums, civic centers, coliseums, etc., providing entertainment and sporting activities, as well as casinos, are usually handicapped accessible, providing adequate seating and accessibility for the disabled, and sometimes at reduced costs. As a matter of fact, this is now mandated under ADA (which will be discussed more fully in the "freedom" need domain section). So, a specific disability is usually served and represented by an organization or multiple organizations for that disability. For example, there is United Cerebral Palsy (UCP) and all of its local and state chapters for people with cerebral palsy, and the American Foundation for the Blind (AFB) for people who are blind and visually impaired, the National Head Injury Foundation for people with traumatic brain injury, the Arthritis Foundation, and so on. If you are uncertain whether there is such an organization that has a special interest and serves your disability, contact the local United Way or even go to the library. You can even contact your local newspaper and inquire or look into special topics sections such as "Community Calendars" or "What's Going On." If you are blind or disabled in any other way and are eligible for the Library of Congress, you can apply for their services and use their equipment including audio tape recorders and audio tape cassettes and they will also look up books of special interest and topics for you including recreational activities for the disabled. The Recording for the Blind (RFB) located in Princeton, New Jersey may also assist here, although this agency serves only the blind and visually impaired. The major issue is, however: Be aggressive and keep looking and then try to connect with a representative of an organization that might be able to assist you either by providing information or providing direct services. Once you have connected with such a representative, cultivate that relationship, either by telephone or in person, be friendly, nonthreatening but assertive (go back to the solution exercises). Also, keep in mind that there are many entities, including local businesses, not typically used by the disabled that can be very helpful with respect to recreational activities. With a good sense of humor, but in all seriousness, I have literally hounded countless numbers of vendors and other businesses that I needed them to help me with special equipment such as electronic equipment to go skiing and waterproof equipment for my hearing aids. Retailers don't seem to mind a bit as long as I am courteous, patient, and communicate well (with assertiveness).

Appendix B

Resources That Address the Psychosocial Need for Freedom

A preliminary comment is very important here. Perhaps even more significantly than the other psychosocial needs, freedom is not only a psychological state but perhaps even more significantly a process of being; that is, a process of expressing freedom and creativity as well as being free. It is important to understand that the opposite state of freedom, entrapment and confinement, is perhaps the most attractive of all the other negative psychosocial states (boredom, low self-worth and feelings of rejection and inadequacy). Anyone who has read Erich Fromm's *Escape from Freedom* can understand this principle more readily. The basis for this positive neuro-association with this negative state of confinement and entrapment is that, for many, these conditions also provide a sense of security in the same sense that a prison cell can provide a sense of security to many prisoners who have no idea how to handle their freedoms and responsibilities, as well as mental institutions providing a sense of security for patients who also do not handle freedom and the responsibilities that go along with it. Freedom, without a sense of self-worth and control over one's life, can signify to many a negative state of isolation and loneliness; hence the precious gift of freedom must be coupled with the willingness to grow and develop physically and psychosocially in order to truly appreciate this highly existential state of being. Our previous discussion of interdependence makes a sharp and clear reference that no man is truly and totally free, that some form of reference group is necessary to survive physically and psychosocially, otherwise they will perish physically or mentally (through craziness). While overconformity through a larger social group or norm may possibly be destructive to individual freedom and expression and inhibit the important psychosocial need, some degree of conformity is necessary for survival. I believe that this "essential conformity" is best actualized and expressed through love and respect for others, including their freedom and their differences that are expressed throughout that very freedom. Everybody has a basic job to do in this world and that is to develop and grow into maturity with increasing skills and competencies to meet their own physical and psychosocial needs. Some go farther than others. In fact, some are very delayed in this process for reasons which go far beyond our human comprehension and knowledge, yet none of us have the right or power to judge that progress or lack of it, but only to respect it, where it is at that given moment in time. Thus, freedom is not a privilege or a gift that is given to us like a packaged present, but rather a right and a responsibility that involves commitment, work, and growth. Basically, it is a process of maturing into our own being that enables us to achieve greater and flexible control over meeting our own needs by respecting the rights and needs of others. Freedom, like morality, cannot be given but must be acquired and learned starting from the day we are born through the university of life. Thus, entities that provide opportunity and advocacy for freedom are not bearers of gifts and laws that protect man's basic freedom and are not insurers that guarantee that freedom will be curtailed. The basic responsibility of freedom is within the individual and it is his responsibility to insure that he embraces freedom primarily by embracing the concept of growth into this world; as seeing this world not as a negative threatening place to be feared, but rather, a joyous opportunity for life. I have been concerned, frankly, very concerned, that for far too long many minorities, the disabled included, have been voicing a militant-like demanding battle cry that they be given their freedom. While it can be argued that there may even be something healthy about this type of demanding approach, a necessary first step in the embryonic stages of development of the disabled as a social class, I wish to caution about the overuse of this type of demanding, threatening approach simply because it can be highly counterproductive. Freedom is a process which emanates from the heart and radiates throughout our society as a whole, rather than the other way around; that is, a gift given from society to the individual. With that in mind, the best approach to the practice of freedom, in essence the removal of physical, psychological, and social barriers for the disabled individual, is a non-threatening solution-focused approach emphasizing empowerment through an internal locus of control. Remember, we may not be able to change every barrier exactly the way we wish to, but we have control over our own physical and mental states; that is the ability to acquire the satisfaction of our physical and psychosocial needs in alternative ways despite the community and social barriers that confront us. Thus, a friendly, parliamentary and nonthreatening approach to resolving barriers that violate our basic sense of freedom not only will be likely to be more productive, but enhance our own sense of control over our physical and mental states. However, firmness and assertiveness should not be sacrificed even within the parameters of a nonthreatening conciliatory approach, and the bottom line is there are laws which protect your freedom and entities which provide enforcement for these laws, and it is up to the consumer to insure that the basic provisions of these laws are carried out otherwise they are only "ropes and sand." If there is any disabled individual finding himself or herself confronted with a substantial degree of idle time (which should not be the case), that individual would be doing himself or herself, as well as the disabled community, a great favor by making every effort possible to learn more about the laws and the entities that support it and enforce it. A new important landmark legislation has recently been passed, the Americans With Disabilities Act (ADA), which guarantees and protects the freedom of all disabled individuals in this country, but it would be useless unless the disabled community, their families, their advocates, and other interested individuals get involved with the understanding, learning, and enforcement of the Act. A smaller version of the ADA has been passed with the Rehabilitation Act of 1973, which essentially is Section 504 of that Act which basically insured that no barriers would exist in federal agencies or any agency receiving federal funding. Unfortunately, 504 became almost a joke simply because there was not substantial consumer involvement by the disabled consumer community and their advocates. We cannot afford to let this happen with ADA.

1. Americans With Disabilities Act (ADA)—This landmark legislation passed on July 21, 1990 has basically five titles, or sections, which basically address five distinct, but interrelated, civil rights issues for the disabled. Enforcement of this Act is to be effective from a three year to a five year period from the date of passage of the Act, depending on the provisions of each title. The purpose of this description and oversimplified summarization is to give you a basic overview, without any intention of giving detailed, accurate facts of the Act. To do so would be impossible given the limitations of this book, but I urge you to check with the appropriate authorities and enforcement entities to get such detailed facts.

Title I basically deals with issues of employment for the disabled. Basically, Title I prevents and protects disabled individuals from discrimination with any aspect of employment, whether it be looking for a job, applying for a job, or obtaining a job and personnel benefits after being employed, if appropriate. Basically, Title I mandates that employers cannot discriminate in the hiring of disabled individuals and must make accommodations to *primary* job-related responsibilities as long as these accommodations do not create "undue hardship." Obviously, as with any law, language can be vague and subject to interpretation, but the application of common sense is highly recommended in the application of ADA. The enforcement entity for Title I of ADA is the Equal Employment Opportunity Commission (EEOC) and you can obtain information about Title I by contacting either the EEOC in Washington, DC or one of

156

the nearby regional offices in your area. If you are uncertain where your regional EEOC office is, your state vocational rehabilitation program should have that information, and if they seem to be hesitant in supplying that information, contact any client assistance program that is associated with a state VR program. (Again, VR will be more fully discussed in the next appendix.) As I understand it, because of the overload of claims filed and investigations conducted, regional EEOCs are asking states to assist them by having the state use their own statewide discrimination bureau make initial investigations of ADA complaints. For example, in the state of Rhode Island, it is the Human Rights Commission under the state Department of Justice which serves as the regional enforcement agency for initial ADA complaints. Again, check with your VR, CAP, or an independent living program (CIL) in your area to find more information about your own state enforcement agencies.

What Title I basically means is that if you apply for a job and you feel yourself to be more qualified, or even equally qualified as another individual but did not get the job, you can file a complaint. It is my understanding that large companies or corporations (200 or more employees) are being encouraged to develop within their company "alternative dispute resolution" committees which address ADA related complaints before they are turned over to either EEOC or the statewide human rights entity. Equally important, if you have been hired for a job, but reasonable accommodations are not being made (that relate only to your *primary* job responsibilities) or you feel you are being treated unfairly with respect to job benefits, promotional opportunities, and other benefits, you can file a complaint on that ground as well. One of the nice things about ADA is that you can either file a complaint with the state or federal agency (EEOC) or through a private civil suit using your own attorney. If the latter is chosen, ADA provisions insure that attorney fees are covered. I have often heard the ADA jokingly referred to as the "Lawyers Relief Act."

Title II of ADA insures that state and local governments do not discriminate against the disabled with respect not only to employment practices but service provisions as well. In other words, any state or local agency must make all aspects of their services, including hiring practices, accessible to the disabled and remove barriers which inhibit or interfere with services provided to the disabled. Basically, Title II is similar to Section 504 of the Rehabilitation Act (to be discussed in the next section) but covers state and local entities whereas 504 covers federal agencies. It is my understanding that each state is to elect state laws which mandate compliance with the federal ADA and that each state agency or facility is to have an authorized ADA representative or committee. Most states have state agencies or state commissions, appointed by the Governor, address the needs of the disabled, and it is most likely this entity that oversees ADA issues. For example, in the State of Rhode Island, state compliance with ADA has been managed primarily through the Governor's Commission for the Handicapped.

Title III addresses the issues of public accommodations. Basically this means that any entity, commercial or otherwise, which serves the public must be accessible to the disabled and remove barriers as long as this does not create "undo hardships." This covers pizza parlors, local businesses, stores, shops, museums, boarding facilities, and any establishment which is open to and serves the public. Basically, these establishments must provide accommodations to the disabled individual but not necessarily construct expensive and costly handicapped accessible equipment such as automatic doors, elevators, etc. For example, if a blind individual goes to a restaurant, it is not necessary that the restaurant pay for the cost of Braille menus if this is going to create "undo hardship," but they must find some reasonable accommodation such as assisting the patron to a table and reading the menu for them. Also, any establishment that is either going to be newly constructed or renovated will be required to make this new construction or renovation barrier free and accessible in accordance with the ADA Guidelines (ADAG).

The enforcement entity for this title on the federal level is the Department of Justice. The statewide Departments of Justice and Attorney General's offices are the enforcement entities on the state level. You can call your State Attorney General's office to get complete and accurate information on ADA and your state's compliance laws and regulations with respect to ADA.

Titles IV and V (there are five titles in ADA) deal with transportation, telecommunication devices, and other miscellaneous provisions of ADA. These Titles of the Act deal with a wide range of issues ranging from telecommunications device for the deaf (TDD) to paratransit transportation accommodations for the disabled. Basically, you can learn more about the law and its provisions by contacting your local library, Library of Congress (for the disabled), any statewide government disability commission within your state, your local vocational rehabilitation unit, or a nearby regional center for independent living. You can look in a United Way guide or even your telephone book to find any human service agency with respect to disabilities and get more accurate information on how you can learn about the law. You could even call the U.S. Government Printing Office in Washington, DC to get a copy of the law itself (for a small fee). Statewide Department of Transportation should have information about transportation and paratransit services and telephone companies should have detailed information about TDD and telephone relay systems for the deaf and other hearing and language disabled individuals and their families.

Again, what is perhaps even more critical in understanding the basic provisions of the act is learning how to use it in an effective, solution-focused manner that empowers, rather limits you. Again, this involves a positive attitude and constructive approaches to the use of this Act in order to benefit you to the maximum extent possible. Again, the next ten years will probably determine whether this is in fact a real act or another political rope of sand, and it is entirely up to the consumers and the disabled individuals to see that this Act protects us to the maximum extent possible.

2. Section 504, Rehabilitation Act—Basically, the Rehabilitation Act of 1973 provides funding for statewide vocational rehabilitation and independent living services to individuals with disabilities. (This will be discussed more fully in a later section.) Basically, the provisions of Section 504 are to insure that any entity, public or private, receiving federal funding must be nondiscriminatory toward the disabled and be barrier-free in the provision of its services and benefits. For the most part, Section 504 has been ineffective and weak since it has been largely unchallenged in courts due to lack of the disabled consumer's involvement, but the provision still stands and can be utilized. As a matter of fact, the ADA mandates that either Section 504 or ADA will be imposed depending on which law is stronger (it also makes provisions that if states have their own laws which are stronger than ADA, the state laws will be the official sanctions). Thus, if you feel a school, even a private one receiving federal funding, or an employer who might receive federal funds (such as hospitals), are discriminating against your disability, you can either file through a private civil suit or contact the appropriate federal agency. For example, if you believe there is a Section 504 violation with respect to education, you can contact the U.S. Department of Education.

3. Education of the Handicapped Act—This federal law mandates that all states develop their own laws and compliances with respect to this law which insure that any handicapped or disabled child must receive an education within the public school system to the maximum extent possible. The child must be mainstreamed into the regular classroom and an individualized education plan (IEP) must be utilized. Schools are mandated to pay for required services necessary to complete educational goals defined within an IEP regardless of where those services are provided (in the school or outside of the school). Many communities have parent advocacy groups with respect to this law which serve as overseers and protection for the school's carrying out their responsibilities.

Appendix C

Resources To Address the Psychosocial Need for Self-Confidence and Self-Worth

Without getting too technical or clinical about this, I differentiated earlier about the difference between self-confidence and self-esteem. Here in this appendix we are focusing on self-confidence; that is confidence in our ability to explore, learn, and conduct a variety of tasks in a variety of domains in our life, whether it pertains to the vocational, educational or other identity issues, that is, issues in terms of how we identify ourselves in terms of the contributions that we make to society. Again, we all have a need to feel like we make a contribution, that we count and are important in one way or another with respect to our identity and how we differentiate ourselves from others. On the other hand, self-esteem has more to do with the overall ability to meet our basic physical and psychosocial needs interdependently including the need for self-worth as well as fun, freedom, and love and belonging. Self-esteem has more to do with how we value ourselves overall. Thus, resources that are more likely to help us with our sense of self-confidence and self-worth, with respect to this book, are likely to be vocational and educational resources whereas resources facilitating the positive development of self-esteem are more likely to be mental health, family service, and other entities which provide overall psychosocial enrichment and growth. On matters of practicality, however, because of their similarity and overlap (despite the distinction), I will list both types in this appendix but with a clear distinction that those vocational and educational entities relating more specifically to one specific psychosocial need; whereas, the mental health, family service, and other psychosocial counseling entities relate more to overall psychosocial maturation.

1. State Vocational Rehabilitation Agencies—Each state has basically a different name for their federally mandated state vocational rehabilitation unit. In Rhode Island it is called the Office of Rehabilitative Services, in Massachusetts it is called the Massachusetts Rehabilitation Commission. Whatever they are called, they are basically state agencies that are usually funded by the federal government through the U.S. Department of Education, Rehabilitation Services Administration (RSA) to provide funds to states providing vocational rehabilitation services. Basically, vocational rehabilitation services provide to the state entities services that enable a disabled individual to acquire a job. Services range from intangible services such as counseling to tangible and durable services such as special equipment. Depending on each state, eligibility for services usually depends on the medical documentation of a disability and, in the case where dollars for special equipment are being requested, financial eligibility as well. When an individual applies for vocational rehabilitation services and is declared to be eligible, a vocational goal is established and every step is elucidated to determine what is necessary to accomplish that goal. Whatever goal and steps are decided, the state vocational rehabilitation unit will assist in the provision of these services necessary to acquire the goal. A goal is defined in terms of a specific job; for example, a clerk typist or social worker, rather than a vague generalized job area such as human services, etc.

"The beauty of vocational rehabilitation agencies is that they have, in the wake of the American With Disabilities Act (ADA) and the Independent Living movement, become increasingly consumer oriented. That is, the client is having more to say and is more directly involved in the rehabilitation process. Years ago the VR programs used to be based on the medical model, that is the big shot, authoritative counselor used to tell the client what is best for the client and if the client didn't follow the advice, he or she would most likely be labeled as a difficult client and not provided services."

If you are uncertain of the name of the vocational rehabilitation unit in your state but desire more information about your vocational rehabilitation unit, you can contact the general information number for your state government, or any school or mental health counselor would know the name. In fact, there are hundreds of ways you can find out the title, such as through the library, United Way, or even a direct call to Washington and ask for the general information number for the Rehabilitation Services Administration under the U.S. Department of Education.

2. Colleges, Schools and Other Educational Institutions—Most schools, public or private, have special student services for individuals with disabilities. They provide information and services which facilitate a disabled individual's ability to acquire an education within that school setting. Now that ADA is around, all schools are mandated to provide accessible, barrier-free services. In essence, all public schools are mandated to provide barrier-free, nondiscriminatory services to students under Section 504 of the Rehabilitation Act, but it appears that this law is loosely enforced and regulated.

In any event, if you are considering acquiring an education or a new skill and are considering the possibility of returning or entering school to do this, you may wish to contact that particular school's general information office to inquire about special student services for people with disabilities. The services can range from providing readers for blind students to special equipment and other materials necessary to complete educational goals. Remember, these services are not going to be broadcasted very readily and offered on a silver platter, but they are mandated to be provided and it is up to you as a consumer to insure that such services are received. If you do inquire about such services and try to obtain them but run into resistances or other problems, you could contact a center for independent living, your State Attorney General's office (ADA Commission), a statewide commission on the handicapped (Governor's Commission), or a statewide protective and advocacy system if one is available. Usually there are many resources to insure this type of protection to see that such basic educational services are carried out in an accessible and nondiscriminatory manner.

3. Statewide Employment and Training Agencies—Again, in various states these specific departments have different titles. In the State of Rhode Island, it is called the Department of Employment and Training. It is basically the statewide unit in which unemployment claims are processed and unemployment compensation is provided. These agencies also provide job placement and job locator services. Specifically for the disabled, usually within the auspices of these departments, they have specific job training and job placement services which provide for incentives for employers to hire disabled and other disadvantaged individuals. The "OJT" or On-the-Job Training Program usually provides employers with subsidies when they hire disabled individuals; that is, if an employer hires a disabled individual under the OJT program, the program typically would pay for fifty percent of the employee's salary (disabled individual) for the first three to six months. You can find out information about these and related programs through either contacting your state employment and training bureau or your state vocational rehabilitation unit.

4. Family Service Agencies and Mental Health Centers—These agencies usually provide services which facilitate the development of overall positive self-esteem. They provide individual and couple counseling to help with problems of self-esteem, as experienced through anxiety, depression, or relationship problems with significant others. Most family service agencies are funded by the United Way and you can call your local United Way to find out about a local family service agency in your area. They have a wide variety

of titles, but usually have the words "family service" in their titles. For example, in Rhode Island there is Child and Family Services of Newport County, Family Services, Inc., and Family Services of Pawtucket. Mental health centers are similar to family service agencies but they focus more on the mental health needs of the community. In the mid-50s, a community mental health movement became popular to help deinstitutionalize individuals from long term hospital and institutional settings. You can learn about your local mental health center by either contacting United Way or even a call to a local hospital should be able to tell you where your local mental health center is since, many times, they have to refer emergency patients there. These agencies are usually nonprofit and base their fees on a sliding scale and are required to be accessible and nondiscriminatory for the disabled. In my observation, too few people have used these resources and it is very unfortunate since they are great resources for helping people to develop better self-esteem and greater control over their lives.

Comments: Once again, there are many resources out there to help the disabled with their needs for self-worth and self-esteem but the important issue is how the resource is used. If you would really like to change, to have the quality of your life become improved, you will approach these services and acquire them with a high degree of motivation, seriousness, and follow through on these services. Through the cultivation of a positive relationship with your therapist, you will be provided with a new opportunity to learn how to foster positive, trustworthy relationships in the wider community and this is crucial for people with disabilities. You may consider that if you begin to find reasons, or, more accurately, excuses, why the counseling sessions at these agencies aren't working out, such as transportation, financial, or relationship problems with the therapist, you may want to ask yourself if you really want to change and make the quality of your life better for you. It is crucial for the positive counseling experience that you begin to make positive neuro-associations with the stresses and difficulties associated with getting to the therapist's office and developing a positive relationship with the therapist. If you feel the agency or therapist is truly not doing their share, it is entirely up to you to assert this point to them and explore it for further clarification for its validity or lack of it. But one thing I do know about therapists, being a psychotherapist myself, is that they expect their clients to work and change doesn't come without work, but you can make this a joyful labor. I remember once reading in Scott's textbook *The Road Less Traveled* that he described two associated characteristics with love and the loving relationship: 1) work and 2) making a commitment. In other words, a loving relationship is one that involves work; that is, positive efforts towards communication, sharing, support, give and take, and the commitment to work on the relationship. This is very true with respect to the relationship with your therapist or any other helping person, for that matter.

If there is only one section from this book you can recall a year or two from now, this is the part I hope you remember. These agencies and policies, including ADA, Title I (a title which deals with employment), are opportunities to acquire meaningful work, and their effectiveness is only as strong as you make it. These entities are *means* for employment, not ends in themselves. It is the attitude and positive approach (an empowerment approach) that makes a difference. Do you really desire to acquire employment or training? You should be thinking of the benefits to the employer. Ask yourself, "What can I provide that will interest them, or what services or skills do I have that will benefit them?" It is my overwhelming impression that far too many people with disabilities simply expect a disabled organization or law to take care of their situations; that is, it is up to them to find you a job, and if they can't they are to blame. This is one of the most negativistic attitudes possible and only will lead to self defeating, disappointing frustrations. As in all aspects of your life in fulfilling your needs, perhaps even more important with employment, your goals should be clear and clarified, making them attainable through the use of small but distinct steps towards those goals, that is, *action steps*. Rather than having a goal of just signing up with the vocational rehabilitation agency, or, on the opposite spectrum, getting a specific job within a specific period of time (that is out of your control and will inevitably set you up for disappointment), your goal should be more related to doing everything within your power to get the job you want or the kind of job you want. You have no control over whether the employer will actually hire you, but you do have control of putting the best possible effort into researching employment opportunities, evaluating your skills and potential skills through the best means possible (including the reading of such books as *What Color is Your Parachute*, putting together the best resume, getting on the phone to set up appointments, and making the best presentation possible for an employment interview. In other words, you can make a full-time job with a highly positive approach in looking for a job and marketing yourself in a manner that undoubtedly will attract the employer. If you cannot do this at the present time, find a way to develop a skill that will make you able to do this. Make positive neuro-associations with this work, make it meaningful, and make it fun. If you do not get hired, or fail to acquire the work you want to, do not get discouraged because your goals are not to actually acquire a job but to put the best possible effort into getting one.

Remember that the employment goal that you choose is not only going to fulfill you need for self-worth, but it is also going to address some of your other needs as well, such as the need for fun, creativity, and belonging. After the employment objective is established, begin to break the objective down in to small action steps, and take action immediately on that first step getting on track with an empowerment reframing of a positive physical and mental focus. This self-empowerment is going to project and emanate from you and have a positive impact on anybody who relates to you, including potential employers and personnel officials. When people apply for jobs, the way a person projects themselves is perhaps more important and at least equally important as what is down on paper such as degrees, previous experience, etc. There is no guarantee that what you do will get you a job (again, that is out of your control) but there is a guarantee that if you don't project yourself and empower yourself to the fullest degree possible you will not get a job.

My belief is that everyone has something to contribute to this society and that contribution can be marketable. As a matter of fact, I do not simply believe this, I know it to the extent that I would bet my life on it. As far as I am concerned, it is one of the greatest and tragic wastes of human resources, families, schools, and the community not to aspire this belief and cultivate it in every person in this country who is old enough to work. Even if a person cannot get a job right away due to lack of employment opportunities and a poor job market, people could be doing so much more with their idle time even if they marketed their skills on a volunteer basis. Time and time again, as director of the nation's first program to provide professional psychosocial counseling to disabled individuals on a community based level, I have ached for people to help, people to read, people to type and use the word processor, people to help run errands, people to interpret, and countless other necessary tasks. I thought about people in nursing homes, people collecting unemployment, people collecting disability and SSI, people on welfare and perhaps countless other people who had undoubtedly millions of hours that they could have put together for their benefit and the benefit of the community. Anybody can contribute and, not only that, anybody can contribute and make a positive, joyous association with that by acquiring a sense of contribution (self-worth), a sense of belonging, and a sense of enjoyment. Even if no job is available, volunteering at a place of employment which is related with your employment goal could be a crucial first step for it not only provides learning opportunities, but demonstrates to employers that

168

you are motivated and provides an opportunity to demonstrate your unique skills and competencies.

Now, consistent with the reality that there is no guarantee that you will get a job even if you do everything you possibly can in a perfect manner (but this is extremely unlikely) and that you are guaranteed not to get a job if you don't put your best effort forward, what I am now about to emphasize is crucial. Do not become dismayed and discouraged by the failure to acquire a job or your employment objective, and more importantly **DO NOT GIVE UP.** Perseverance is crucial. If you remind yourself that your goal is to do the best you possibly can, you will not be as easily discouraged. But the reality for anyone is that success only comes after repeated failure (fail to acquire the job outcome). Take a look at one of John Grisham's books in the preface and acknowledgments where he thanks his literary agent for his number one best selling book *The Firm* because the agent refused to give up and finally found a publisher who would publish his book. Jack Nicholson, at his first Academy Award reception when he won an Oscar for his performance in *One Flew Over the Cuckoo's Nest*, thanked all of those people who previously snubbed him in his rising acting career because it gave him the motivation to go and show people what he could do. In other words, he changed the meaning of his failures as renewed, determined efforts to succeed. Even athletes who acquire the best percentages fail more than they succeed. Babe Ruth had more strikeouts than anyone (or at least more than the vast majority of other sluggers) and Dan Marino, famed quarterback of the Miami Dolphins, threw literally thousands of interceptions (unsuccessful passes) although he was one of the leading touchdown passers. I proudly display my three Gold Medals in Alpine competition, having been a member of the U.S. Disabled Ski Team, but what most people don't realize is the number of physically and psychologically painful wipeouts and gate crashes I have accumulated and I even once destroyed a time clock at the finish line of a race. People jokingly referred to the fact that I must like to chew bamboo since I was eating so much of it wiping out in race courses. I wrote several winning proposals, including the front runner to the U.S. Government for the Department of Education. Many of the first ones I submitted were undoubtedly laughed at by the peer reviewers because they were written so incompetently. But it was essential that I change my perspective and put this failure into a new meaning and looked at it as a positive learning opportunity, as well as using a great deal of humor. I just kept reminding myself that my goal was to do everything I possibly could to obtain satisfaction with that and let the outcome fall into place as it inevitably would.

Appendix D

Resources That Address the Psychosocial Need for Love and Belonging

This obviously is a crucial resource because it not only meets one of our psychosocial needs, but it also serves as the basis for the third major psychosocial issue in successfully resolving the grieving process with respect to a physical loss or a disabling condition; that is, developing adequate and healthy systems of support. The first thing I would like to point out is that there are countless books on the subject which relate to cultivating and fostering positive and mature relationships including helping relationships. One that stands out in my mind, however, is a classic which is short and easy to read. It is written by Eric Fromm and called *The Art of Loving*. While this book outlines the general characteristics of a true loving relationship, one of the major points it emphasizes is that most people are in the receptive, immature state of desiring to be loved rather than to give love. We have probably all heard this a million times, yet it is so true, and that is the best way to get love is to give it. In fact, this relates to about anything. If we want something, the best way to get it is to give it.

Nevertheless, the art of cultivating healthy, nurturing relationships is primarily centered on clear, effective communication. The true basis of healthy communication is not necessarily a good grasp of your native language with a good vocabulary and good grammar skills (although this is certainly very helpful), but rather a clear sense of empowerment and self-esteem within yourself. When you feel a sense of basic empowerment and self-esteem, that is, a sense of having control over meeting your physical and psychosocial needs interdependently with an internal locus of control, it eliminates the desire and motive to control and manipulate others through deceptive and manipulative types of communication styles. Thus, although entities will be listed here that can facilitate the need for developing relationships, continuous work on your personal growth is imperative. There are thousands of resources that can help with this including mental health agencies, family service agencies as well as other psychosocial resources, including private psychotherapists (psychiatrists, clinical social workers, psychologists). These agencies and resources also provide support groups to assist with personal growth and offer unique "here and now" opportunities for social interaction allowing for the cultivation of positive communication skills with the guidance of a skilled group leader or psychotherapist. Once again, remember that the development of these interpersonal skills not only leads to the increased likelihood of more intimate, satisfying relationships, but improvement in other areas as well, including job opportunities since communication skills are so important for successful employment outcomes.

Another thing to keep in mind is that joining informal and formal groups centered around topics of interest (such as clubs, workshops, educational centers, etc.) provides opportunity for developing relationships within shared areas of interest. Many adult clients I have had in psychotherapy who have busy schedules and only a few extra hours available for social opportunities felt that they were limited to restaurants and taverns which served alcoholic beverages as the only possibilities for meeting new people, including people of the opposite sex. But I reminded them that cultivating their own personal activities and interests could be even more effective since it would provide opportunities to join clubs, enter training programs related to that interest, or find other sources of group activities connected to these interests.

With respect to disabilities, I think it can be highly helpful to find consumer groups which share your disability or some aspect of your disability. These groups obviously serve a wide range of useful purposes including the exchange of valuable information as well

172

as raising money for disability research and rehabilitation, but I believe one of the most valuable assets is the type of peer support they actually supply or could potentially supply. I am going to give an overview of a variety of disability groups of which I am aware, but this overview may be outdated in some cases and it certainly is not exhaustive. The intent is to help you either discover the consumer group that you can connect to or perhaps even provide you with the incentive of developing such a group within your area or even regionally. Most of these groups provide support groups and I have spoken at, literally, hundreds of these groups and found them to be invaluable. I am not implying they are perfect, for no group is, and, certainly, some may have their problems, but these problems, once again, can be faced with a positive attitude and a solution-focused approach in terms of dealing with them.

Examples of these Disability Groups, including self-help groups are The National Head Injury Foundation, National Diabetes Association, The Arthritis Foundation, The Multiple Sclerosis Society, Muscular Dystrophy Foundation, The American Heart Association, The American Cancer Society, The Spinal Cord Injury Foundation, Commission For the Deaf and Hard of Hearing (Washington, D.C.), and the like. With respect to your particular disability, regardless of its origin [accident, illness, aging], there most likely is a national organization with a state chapter and/or affiliates. If you cannot locate these in your telephone book, your local United Way Agency or through any other means, you definitely will be able to find some reference in your local library.

Centers for Independent Living is also a great resource for developing relationships among other disabled and advocates. As stated earlier these organizations, funded under Title VII of the Rehabilitation Act provide four core services including peer support. They can also be used as an informal network to find other resources with respect to social interest and recreation.

Conclusion

The intent here with listing and identifying these resources which may facilitate satisfaction of one or more of the psychosocial needs (I deliberately used the word "may" since it is up to you) is not to provide an exhaustive, complete list, of course, because the resources I have outlined do not even make a dent in all the possible resources that are out there that could benefit the disabled. The intent is to get you thinking and motivated about cultivating such resources on your own as well. The major issue is that you get positioned to take action now to explore, cultivate, and utilize such resources. If necessary, get on the phone and start making calls. If you have problems using the phone, find out a way to correct this problem that is accommodating to your disability or otherwise. Go to these places or have a representative come to you. Start making connections now. You are the only one who can possibly satisfy your needs and empower your life. You can perhaps manipulate other people to take partial control of your needs through such manipulative maneuvers as guilt provocation or overt demands, but this will, in the end, fall far short of total needs satisfaction. Regardless of the extent and type of your limitation, there are ways to meet your needs and there is a definite possibility to develop an overall positive sense of self-esteem. The steps outlined in this book were designed to show you how to do that, directly by yourself and within you control, and although it may include the help of other people, that help is offered because they want to help you because of the way you interact with them. Meeting your physical and psychosocial needs interdependently is your goal, not getting a job that pays a lucrative salary, or developing an intimate relationship that could lead to a wife/husband and children, since these are only means to needs satisfaction and therefore possibilities, rather than ends in themselves. I know many people who are extremely wealthy and many people who are married with children and yet are quite unhappy with their low level of needs satisfaction and poor self-esteem resulting from an external locus of control in attempting to get their needs satisfied. I also know a woman who is born totally paralyzed, unable to move or speak because of a rare birth condition and yet, step by step, with the assistance of computerized technology and a caring professional, is now fully employed, and earning $500.00 for each speech she gives to the countless audiences who solicit her. Once she was only able to communicate by pointing her gaze at a letterboard. But because of her positive attitude assisted by computerized technology she is able to communicate effectively and, much more importantly, satisfy all of her needs interdependently. In whose shoes would you rather be—hers or the unhappy millionaire's or the unhappily married people's? Think about it.

Whatever particular mental and/or physical activity you choose to fulfill your need for fun and enjoyment it is crucial that you be thorough and creative in the search and utilization of resources (including technological adaptive devices) that will accommodate for your disability. It is important that you explore all existing resources and, if something does not exist to your satisfaction, you will want to find ways to design and manufacture such adaptive resources, or at least have others knowledgeable and skilled in that area manufacture such a device. The thoroughness in this investigative research and creativity can be facilitated not only by a positive, solution-focused attitude, but an attitude that includes a sense of humor. For example, I not only enjoy water skiing as a recreational activity but I also compete annually at an event sponsored by the American Blind Water Skiers Association in Orlando, Florida as well as another event sponsored by American Water Ski Association (AWSA). I decided that I would enjoy the sport more and could perhaps benefit more from a coaching perspective if I were able to hear better at least while I was in the water after the boat had stopped. After exploring a wide variety of resources including electronic retailers as well as the U.S. Navy (Naval Underwater Systems), I learned that there was a waterproof hearing aid available that was manufactured by a Japanese company and distributed in the United States by a firm that was located in Bristol, Pennsylvania. After contacting the United States distributor, I was able to successfully work out an exchange in which I would promote their product if they would let me use it. However, I learned that although the hearing aids were basically waterproof, their waterproof capability was more suitable for less rigorous activity such as swimming and bathing but for the more challenging activities of water skiing, which often included hard wipeouts, the waterproof capability was not total since the hearing aid often would disassemble and accumulate water after a hard contact with the water surface. Thus, after more exploration, I learned that there were actual waterproof condoms available, rubberized devices which would roll over and protect most of the aid except for the crucial, highly sensitive microphone which was left exposed. Since the specialized hearing aid condom would not completely do the job, I then decided to become creative and take actual, prophylactic condoms commercially dispensed in drugstores and use those as well. This conventional condom, being larger in size, allowed me to deposit the aid into it above the microphone and then to secure the condom tightly around the hook of the hearing aid, located above the microphone but below the ear mold, with a strong, thin fish line. Thus, I was able to take an existing device and find adaptive methods of increasing its waterproofing capability to suit my needs and I am able to enjoy water skiing while actually being able to hear to the maximum extent that my hearing limitations will allow me. I am now in the process of exploring the additional devices that will enable me to communicate with people who are actually on the boat while I am skiing such as a walkie-talkie or FM system. Of course, the challenge is, once again, to find ways of making such a device waterproof, but I am convinced that it is possible and I am equally convinced that I will find that method. The major point that I am making is that a positive solution-focused approach is necessary here as well as a strong sense of perseverance. I could have easily given up after the first unsuccessful attempt, but the persistence enabled me to explore a wide variety of options and eventually come up with a successful solution. On top of it all, the condoms standing out behind my ear are a humorous sight and offer more than ample opportunity for conversations other than just about water skiing. I also make the same approach with my winter skiing activities. I have been successful with the use of personalized FM system so that I can follow my guide easier, but I have also adapted a second backup system so that my guide can hear me clearly. Since the frequency does not allow for a range to communicate beyond fifty yards or so, I am now in the process of exploring for a device that will enable me to separate from my guide for a distance of about 300 to 500 yards, so that he (my guide) can stand on top of a major slope and just simply guide me through the walkie-talkie without actually having to ski. We have tried a range of other assistive devices including bright lights, reflective tape, and other adaptive gadgets which have, at times, appeared hilarious and were colossal flops, but I never would have known if they were flops unless they were actually tried. I often wondered how often the Wright brothers flopped before they were able to successfully design and use an air soaring vehicle. The gist of all of this is, once again, that the goal is shifting your efforts and letting the successful outcome fall into place. This means that if I tried everything within my power and within my range of knowledge and creativity to find solutions to the problems and challenges that confronted me, I would not only be likely to find such an option, but could also actually take great enthusiasm and even joy in the exploration and process of a successful solution outcome. Once again, it is a difference between accomplishing to become satisfied versus satisfyingly accomplishing something. By the way, this process not only enables us to find more options to satisfying our need for fun, but certainly our other needs as well (as explained before). This creative process certainly fulfills the need for freedom because, in a very real sense, the unknown is being explored. I truly believe it is this pursuit of exploring the unknown to make it known is one of the greatest needs of human beings, a need that makes the exploration of life worth living in itself. Think of it this way. If you had all the money and things in the world you wanted and, thus, could easily accomplish any goal you wished to, would life truly be satisfying? I truly believe the need for freedom sets the basis for searching and exploring, in a creative manner, into the unknown that transcends us beyond the limits of our self-centered ego boundaries. What I simply mean by this is that it is in this creative process of exploration that we lose consciousness of ourselves including the boundaries that limit us almost as if we lost an altered state of consciousness without the anxiety producing sensation of feeling lost. It is this altered state of consciousness's positive creativity from which we often snap out of, almost as if we had been entranced, and become aware of ourselves and our senses provide invaluable clues to our very essence and these experiences should be encouraged for yourself since they are the very heart of solution-focused, empowerment approaches. I have often thought that there would be far fewer problems in this world if this type of individualistic experience were encouraged on a grander social scale and, since disabled people have so many challenges to confront, the creative consciousness of the disabled is one manner in which new meaning can be given to the disability and the grieving process. Furthermore, from a collective viewpoint, it is a basis in which disabled people could be influential in actually contributing to the larger society as a group simply by reminding the larger society that creativity is one of the major purposes of life itself for, in a sense, creativity is life. Thus, this creative solution-focused approach embedded in the genuine sense of empowerment is not only a search for practical solutions to practical problems in living, but a way of life in itself, a way of living and being.